Cindy's stror

approach tak

life. Through

as she continues to stand on His Word. You will find her humor and practical approach a plus as you read and learn from *I Thought I Heard the Lion's Roar*. I believe this book will be a great blessing to you.

—Duane Vander Klok, Sr. Exec. Pastor,
Resurrection Life Church

I Thought I Heard the Lion's Roar is a practical approach to bring God into your everyday difficulties. By sharing her own family's journey through tough times, Cindy Allen enlightens her readers to biblical truths that break the power of fear and failure.

—Robert E Bogard, Exec. Pastor
Adult Ministries, Gateway Church

Having known Cindy and Jim very intimately since 1988, we can truly attest that this is really her! A woman of valor and true character and willing to take on the devil at any time and at any level. This couple lives a life of faith in Jesus Christ that is amazingly commendable. Their witness to us and to the whole world rarely goes unnoticed. The wonderful way that Cindy has penned her experiences will be a tremendous faith boost to anyone who may need a realignment in our Lord Jesus. This read is mostly about living in victory every day even when things look bleak and faith just wants to give up. Pick it up and enjoy.

—Pastors Ray and Joyce Townsend,
Sparta United Methodist Church

I Thought I Heard the Lion's Roar is a refreshing account of experiencing victory through the difficult times that life brings. Standing on the Word of God and listening to His voice are the keys that bring blessing, strength, and peace to everyday situations. This book is both practical and reveals the extraordinary nature of God and his blessings when we follow Him. A must-read.

—Pastors Joe and Cindy Tucker,
Resurrection Life Church

I was honestly encouraged with my current season about staying close to God instead of letting my own thinking figure everything out. I loved it…I think it is a practical life lesson. Everyone will relate to all of it or part of it; there is something for everyone. I pray the Lord uses it to encourage all of us who find ourselves overwhelmed, a little scared, and unsure of the future. It's a great testimony and done with good taste and humor!

—Kathy Wylie, Exec. Assistant,
Resurrection Life Church

This book is just so amazing and such a help when you hear the lions roar in your life, and we have all heard it at one time or another. I personally needed to hear all these things that Cindy has written about and would recommend it to everyone to read. I can't wait for her second edition to come out. I am proud to call her my friend. She has helped me in years past with struggles in my own life. I thank her for her strong faith and love.

—Sally Edmunds, Book Reviewer

I didn't know that I've ever known anyone as strong-willed and strong in faith as Cindy Allen. As I read *I Thought I Heard the Lion's Roar*, I found myself finding many times that I would have thrown up my hands and said, "I give up." At least that's what would probably have happened before reading this inspiring book of faith. Cindy Allen has given me, as well as everyone who reads her book, the references needed to help us fight the battles we are faced with when we "hear the lion's roar."

—Martha Cheves, Author

I Thought I Heard the Lion's Roar shares some very personal and dramatic events. Cindy is exquisite and loving, but she's also in your face with no holding back when it comes to her core values, her belief in the one true God, Jesus Christ, and she has no shame holding back her thoughts or opinions. A great mix of drama, advice, and humor. Trolls, chocolate, and hair-raising statements are no stranger to this gal. Cindy's advice is sound and firm, yet encouraging. She always leads you back to relying on God's Word no matter the storm your weathering. For a motivational and encouraging read, this will lift your spirits and brighten your hopes to the sun that will set on your horizon.

—Tina Bennett, Tina's Book Reviews

I Thought I Heard the Lion's Roar (Second Edition)

I Thought I Heard the Lion's Roar (Second Edition)

A Hindsight Diary to Help You Discern the Voice of God in Turbulent Times

Cindy Brubaker Allen

TATE PUBLISHING
AND ENTERPRISES, LLC

Published by Tate Publishing & Enterprises, LLC
127 E. Trade Center Terrace | Mustang, Oklahoma 73064 USA
1.888.361.9473 | www.tatepublishing.com

Tate Publishing is committed to excellence in the publishing industry. The company reflects the philosophy established by the founders, based on Psalm 68:11,
"The Lord gave the word and great was the company of those who published it."

Cover design by Jim Villaflores
Interior design by Richell Balansag

Published in the United States of America

ISBN: 978-1-63122-367-9
1. Religion / Christian Life / Inspirational
2. Religion / Christian Life / Spiritual Warfare
16.01.12

This book is dedicated to the Lord and my husband Jim—without both, I would not have this story to tell. My life is a testament to the faithfulness of a loving God and husband. I also want to dedicate this story to all those longing to hear God's voice in their own lives. He has great plans for you.

Acknowledgments

Every life has a story, but some feel a need to put it in written form. I am very thankful for all those who have helped me compile my thoughts, correct my grammar, and encouraged me to continue and push through all the ups and downs throughout my journey. Though the story is not over, this part is in print and out into your hands because of my family, friends, pastors, coworkers, bosses, and all those who have made my life rich beyond measure. I want to acknowledge and thank those who helped me with this project. First of all my husband and lifelong sweetheart, Jim. Your patience, love, and perseverance have always kept us on our course. I love and honor you. Thank you for giving me our two sons, Ryan and Matt. They are my claim to fame and the straight arrows in my quiver. If I never did another thing, I would be content.

Rebekah and Jenny, my two "daughters-in-love," and our fabulous grandchildren, Joshua, Naomi, Sam and Ellie. You all delight my life with a wonder that only a grandma and mother-in-law can understand. Thank you so much for the sunshine you give me and the heritage Jim and I will leave behind. Many, many thanks go to my mom, stepdad, Dennie, brother, sister, and their families. Though there are not many of us, as my mother often said, "We might be small, but so is a stick of dynamite." Explosive we can be but would lay down our lives for each other in a minute. Even though my dad, Don Brubaker, cheers me on from heavenly grandstands, I thank him so much. He is my forerunner. I love and miss you, but as you would say, "The commission goes on." My extended Allen family and friends at Res. Life and Forest Hill Church, I love you all so very much. You are my support system, and you mean the world to me.

I have so many more to thank, but at the risk of boring my audience, I will close with one last acknowledgment. This one goes to my in-laws. Dick and Jane, you hung in there for Jim and me, always checking the Internet postings for a job for your firstborn son and sending us money even though we never asked, saying, "That's just what family does." The Lord used you to help us, and for that, I will be forever grateful.

Contents

Be sober, be vigilant; because your adversary
the devil walks about like a roaring lion,
seeking whom he may devour.

—1 Peter 5:8 (NKJV)

Foreword

I have heard the roar of the lion—have you? Maybe it came in the form of a betrayal from someone you loved. Perhaps it was hidden behind the words of an employer who told you that your services were no longer needed. Maybe it was disguised in the phone call you received from the doctor saying that he had bad news. I believe we all sometimes hear the lion's roar, though we often fail to recognize it for what it is.

The lion—the one who prowls around seeking "whom he may devour" (1 Pet. 5:8)—wants to paralyze our faith. What we do when we hear him roar makes all the difference in the world. Some books on dealing with the difficulties of life come across as little more than sterile textbooks. Others are so saturated with the author's pain that they offer the reader no substantial help. *I Thought I Heard the Lion's Roar* is different.

Cindy Allen is the real deal, and she holds nothing back as she tells her story. Through life's challenges, she has learned the secret of leaning into God, not away from him, and she has developed a tenacity that makes her faith in God infectious.

Cindy's honest, relatable, and often humorous illustrations help us grasp foundational truths that are essential for living successfully in a world of change. Even though I already knew her story, seeing it in print has encouraged me and reminded me of God's amazing love and faithfulness. I believe that the insights offered in the pages ahead will renew your hope and help you respond appropriately the next time you hear the lion's roar.

—Deb Kirgis
Ministry Director/Associate Pastor
Walking by Faith Television Ministry,
Resurrection Life Church

Introduction

Turbulent times—I never thought those words would come out of my mouth to describe my life. If you have picked up this book, you may have thought the same thing. *When will life ever get back to normal? What is normal anyway?* It's been said that "Normal is just a setting on your dryer," but I now think change is the new normal. Life is full of changes. We resist it and dread it, but in reality normal is gone, and change is here to stay. The only way to stay ahead of the curve is to embrace it. This book is written with the intent to stretch your thinking and embrace the Author of change.

The Bible says the Lord speaks to his children, but are we listening? How many times have you heard or said to yourself, "If they would only just listen!" The word of God says, "And your ears will hear a word behind you, saying, This is the way; walk in it, when you turn to the right hand and when you turn to the left" (Isa. 30:21, TAB). You have actually been programmed to hear God's voice. Unfortunately, we don't understand the program and want to do things our way, on our terms, or in our own time. But by doing it our way, we never fully grasp the wonderful mysteries God has in store for those who will listen to his voice. It is to our benefit to give the Lord our attention and tune our ears to his frequency; he has so much he wants to say to us!

Hopefully, this book will give you some commonsense principles that will help you to discern between all the voices that try to speak into your life, especially during difficult times. We all experience tragedy, loss, guilt, fear, sickness, as well as surprises, success, joy—the list can go on and on. I wrote this book to encourage you. I am a common woman blessed with some common sense, and I think you will be able to relate to my examples and journey. Most things are learned in hindsight, and after reading how God relates to his children, I hope you will be able to identify his voice from all the other voices in your life by using a few simple principles that he has taught me. I also hope you will learn to discern the difference between the roar of the lion's lies (Satan) and the truth of God's word for your life. The Lord knew each and every one of us before we were born. He has a plan and a path for us. He formed and fashioned us before we were born and has our best interest in mind. Let us press on while looking with hindsight to see how to hear the still small voice of God. I have found that most of us have misconceptions of who God is and why he created us. This world and the enemy of your soul has done it's best to distort the truth of what God thinks about you and how you think about him and yourself. It is my hope and belief it's God's desire that you come to understand the depth and breadth of his love for you. So let's kick back, set aside our preconceived notions about how we can or cannot hear the voice of God, and travel with me on a journey that will hopefully give you some concrete steps to recognizing his voice.

Setting the Stage

My husband and I have been married over forty-four years. We are blessed with two wonderful sons, two "daughters-in-love," four grandchildren, mothers, fathers, sisters, brothers, their families, and friends too numerous to count. They are very precious to us, and we could not have gone through this journey without their love, wisdom, and support.

We have been blessed to live in the water-winter wonderland of Michigan—you know, the Mitten State. When anyone asks a Michigander where they are from, we hold up our right hand like taking a pledge and show you right where we live on the mitten of Michigan. Our spot on that mitten was Michigan's great southwest, along the Lake Michigan shoreline. Throughout our marriage, we have had our ups and downs and experienced a lot of stories to tell, but none of them compare to our past fourteen plus years. But first, it is best I give you some background history, which should help you to get to know me better and understand why I feel called to write about our experiences.

I am currently sixty-three years old. My husband, Jim, and I have both been told that we do not look or act our age at all, which I consider a compliment. We have great DNA, proper skin care practices, and we try very hard to take good care of ourselves.

Jim and I were raised in two entirely different ways: he was a city boy, and I was a country girl. My family moved often, and Jim's stayed put. I have a brother, Jeff, ten years younger, who lives in Dallas with his wife, Amy, and their three adorable children. My sister, Terrie, is two and a half years older than me and has been married for forty-three years to Bob and are both pastors in Tampa, Florida. Now, if you have done the math, you have already figured out that I am the middle child. The experts say the middle child is usually more adjusted and seems to go through life a little easier because of their position in the family. I don't know about that, but I have always had a positive attitude toward life and choose to look at the glass as half full instead of half empty. But middle child or not, my childhood was different. As a family, we were always on the move. My father followed the job opportunities, and we followed my father. With each new job came a new location. The boxes would come out, and we would start over again.

I found out that all those moves and disruptions affected me profoundly. When you move frequently, that also means changing schools (eight that I can remember) and even more homes because sometimes we moved several times during a school year as well as lived in different states. That can be hard on a kid. I would just get settled and start making some friends, and then the boxes would come out again. After a while, I just kind of gave up on making lasting friendships and did the best I could, always keeping my heart prepared for a vacancy.

My father and mother provided for our family, and the moves were unfortunately the consequences of a lousy economy and lack of employment opportunities, but we managed. We always had each other, and that kept our family together.

My mom and dad were seekers. They were always looking for contentment and completeness. There was this void in their lives, and they sought out different ways to fill it. That search took us on several side trips before we found the God-piece of the puzzle that filled that void. When the traditional church did not answer my father's list of often-unanswerable questions, we were directed to yet another religion. That took us down a slippery slope, which eventually led us to the cult and occult road of destruction. It was during those dark years that I dabbled with the tools of the enemy. For fun, we would play with tarot cards and Ouija boards. By using these tools, we opened the door wide for the enemy of our souls, and he stepped right in.

I was seventeen years old when I met Jim. My sister and I were folksingers at a family campground in Northport, Michigan, and Jim was the cook in the restaurant. It was the late sixties, and I resembled a bit of a flower child. My sister, Terrie, and I traveled around to the different campsites with our guitar and tambourine and led folk songs around the campfires. Jim and I met one night when a bunch of us from the campground traveled to a park overlooking Lake Michigan to watch shooting stars. The sky in Northern Michigan was so clear it felt like you could almost reach out and touch the stars. Jim sat next to me on the picnic table as we prepared to be wowed by the starlit heavens. I honestly did not even notice him at first. Most of the girls, myself included, had our eyes directed on Jim's cousin at the time. But Jim spotted the first shooting star, and as he drew his arm in front of me, showing me the direction of the star's trail, his face came close to my cheek, and his outdoorsy scent caught my attention. At that moment, my head was reeling with a feeling I'd never felt before. *Who is this guy and where did he come from?* That night was the beginning of the rest of my life. Not only did I fall head over heels in love with him, but he was my ticket out of my insecure world.

Jim was the most solid person I knew, even at his young age of nineteen. His family raised him with a strong sense of stability and accountability. He pretty much lived in the same house his whole life, except during the summer months up north where we met. I just could not imagine living in one place for more than a couple of years; that did not seem normal to me. We dated long distance for two years and would talk on the phone every Sunday night for the five-cents-a-minute rate. My mom would say, "Heaven help the person who gets in the way of *that* phone call." It was a long two years apart from each other, with Jim in college and me completing high school and starting junior college. Jim would travel up for a weekend visit every few months, even during some of Northern Michigan's snowiest winters. We believed it was true love at first sight, a summer romance that passed the test of time. We were married in the summer of 1971, after Jim graduated from college—very young, but so much in love. We left our homes with one car filled with our possessions and $250 in cash, heading to Dallas, Texas. Jim landed a good job twelve hundred miles away from home. Even though we lived in Dallas only one lonely year, it was a very good lesson on living on our own and cutting the apron strings. Jim changed jobs, and we moved to Illinois for another four and a half years and then finally landed back in Michigan just shortly before our first son was born determined not to move away from our Mitten State again.

My family's Christian experience began with my dad. He was the first person in our family to be "born again." In 1977, my father went through a horrific experience. He suffered six heart attacks in a two-week period. The doctors called the heart attacks "widow makers," because usually patients do not survive these massive attacks and leave widows in their wake. He was so young to have such an experience, but we were so thankful that he did; our future depended on it. You see, during that time, my father was one of the few people to actually have an out-of-body experience and live to tell about it. His experience was even more different than most because it did not involve the great white light at the end of the tunnel that many spoke of, but a fiery-red eye of death and hell. It was through my father's experiences that he and our whole family were saved. It totally scared the hell out of us.

My mom was the second person in our family to accept the Lord as her personal savior. While she sat in the waiting room at the hospital with her husband almost dying in ICU, she decided to call a prayer line from the old PTL, the *Praise the Lord* club in Fort Mill, South Carolina. My mom's prayer request was for my dad, but the gentleman on the phone said to her, "Never mind about your husband, God knows what he needs.

What about you, young lady?" That day, she gave her life to the Lord and, as an added bonus, was delivered from smoking on the spot, which is a good thing because they don't allow smoking in ICU!

I was the next one in the family to be born again. In the past, as a family, we picked what religion we wanted to believe, kind of like a smorgasbord of beliefs. Heaven, yes. Hell, no thank you. And if we don't do it right the first time, we can come back and have another try, kinda like a Monopoly game for eternity. But after my father's experience, we could no longer package our theories up in a nice little bag of beliefs. It appeared as though someone had already made up the rules and printed them all up in a book called the Bible.

It was a few months before the Christmas of 1979 that I sat down with my dad and confronted him about all the beliefs he had taught me over the years. I asked him about all the religions he taught us, such as karma and reincarnation. "How does that line up with this Jesus of yours?" I asked. "Why should I believe you? Isn't this just another one of your phases?" I was pretty rough on him. My dad bowed his head and, in sincere humility, said, "I was wrong. Everything I taught you was wrong, Cindy." My father *never* admitted that he was wrong. I saw a humility and regret with remorse I'd never seen before. I thought, *There must really be something to this new religion my dad is talking about*. You see, we never thought of ourselves as heathens or "unsaved." We went to church occasionally, read our horoscopes, studied different lines of thinking; and when we prayed, we always prayed for Jesus's sake—but we never knew this Jesus. We understood that Jesus was the Son of God and number two in the Trinity, whatever that meant. On Christmas morning, we celebrated his birthday along with Santa, and on Easter, we celebrated his resurrection and the Easter bunny. It was just another holiday to receive gifts and time off from work.

Christmas Eve 1979 was the end of a life I did not want and the beginning of a life I had always hoped for. I was twenty-seven, our first son, Ryan, was three, and his little brother, Matt, was only six weeks old. My folks were visiting with Jim and me for the Christmas holiday. My father had tried preaching to me, but that only drove me away. So over the next few months, he began to pray and ask the Lord to make himself real to me. On that Christmas Eve, I remember asking my dad three questions about this Jesus of his. I put my old Bible on the table, the one I received from Sunday school years ago, and said, "Show me where it says in this Bible about not eating meat"—we were vegetarians in one of our religions—"and show me where it talks about reincarnation and hell, and thirdly, show me where it says anything regarding your heaven-and-hell experience." (Remember my family didn't believe in hell and were not really sure about heaven either.) I thought those would be tough questions, but Dad gently opened his Bible; and for each question I had, he read a scripture from the word of God.

Number 1: What about eating meat? "Now the Spirit expressly says that in latter times some will depart from the faith, giving heed to deceiving spirits and doctrines of demons, speaking lies in hypocrisy, having their own conscience seared with a hot iron, forbidding to marry, and commanding to abstain from foods which God created to be received with thanksgiving by those who believe and know the truth" (1 Tim. 4:1–3).

Number 2: Reincarnation and hell? "And just as it is appointed for [all] men once to die, and after that the [certain] judgment" (Heb. 9:27, TAB).

Number 3: Explain this out-of-body experience you had. "I know a man in Christ who fourteen years ago –whether in the body I do not know, or whether out of the body I do not know, God knows –such a one was caught up to the third heaven. And I know such a man—whether in the body or out of the body I do not know, God knows—" (2 Cor. 12:2–3, NKJV).

After my dad gave me these scriptures, I said nothing else to him the rest of that evening. I went to bed that Christmas Eve a sinner, and I woke up Christmas morning a sinner saved by grace. During the night, I met with my Savior and asked him into my life. When I realized there was a hell, I turned and ran right into the arms of my Loving Savior, Jesus Christ. Jesus was there with his arms open wide, and heaven became my home for eternity.

Within three short months, Jim recommitted his life to the Lord, and we have been born-again, spirit-filled believers for over thirty-five years now. My life changed dramatically and I absorbed the Bible. I read like I had never read before and actually understood what I was reading. Before this experience, the Bible had been a locked book to me. But now, the words came to life. Things began to make sense to me, and I understood that I was created on purpose, with a purpose. Darkness began to fade away, and the light and love of God's word filled my life with hope and healing. Through the following years, Jim and I raised our young family with the help of God's word. Our little boys accepted Jesus into their hearts at a very young age and were filled with the Holy Spirit. We all grew up in Christ together. Everything Jim and I learned about the Lord and his word was immediately shared with the boys. We were so hungry for God and his way of doing things that life, even though sometimes difficult, was wonderful.

We have a great marriage and a solid grounding in the word of God. We raised our children, now grown, in the admonition of the Lord; and they have made good decisions with their lives, and for that we are blessed. We've also had our tragedies. The death of my father, sickness in our families, financial concerns—the list goes on—but God has always shown himself faithful to us. But even through it all, I do not believe we were prepared for the next season of our lives. However, prepared or not, our season of trial, test, and travail had come. Revelation 12:11 says, "And they overcame him by the blood of the Lamb and by the word of their testimony."

Our Testimony

Fear Not

It was a warm, sunny April day in 2001. I decided to take a walk and talk to the Lord, my constant traveling companion. As I was strolling down our long, tree-shaded driveway, I heard a voice as clear as if someone were walking behind me say, "Fear not." I stopped and took a breath and said, "Of what?" I heard nothing but the leaves rustling in the gentle breeze. Then after long pause, I said, "Lord, your servant is listening." I learned that from Samuel in the Bible. God would whisper Samuel's name, and he would stop and tell the Lord he was listening.

Then I heard it again. "Fear not." I knew this voice; it was as reassuring and soft as the gentle breeze that flows through your hair on a warm spring day. It was my Heavenly Father's voice, and he was alerting me that fear was around the corner, but to not be afraid. As I slowly continued on my walk, the Lord brought to my remembrance what the Israelites did during their captivity in Egypt just before their great Exodus. The plagues were on their way, and the Israelites were to take part in the Passover ceremony. As directed by God, they took their lambs, sacrificed them, and spread the blood over their doorposts so the angel of death would pass by their household. This struck a chord in my heart about what I was to do. I believed the Lord was instructing me to apply the blood of the lamb symbolically over my family. This may sound odd to anyone who does not know about the symbolism of this sacrifice, so let me try and explain. When the Egyptian guards were sent to kill the firstborn of all the Israelites, they ran through the villages doing what they had been commanded to do. However, when they saw the blood of the sacrificed lamb on the doorposts, they passed by because that blood meant death had already been there.

As New Testament Christians, we have the blood of Jesus as our protection. Jesus is the Lamb of God that was sacrificed for us. As Christians, we are to apply his blood symbolically, verbally, over our household and especially when the Lord instructs us to do so. So for the remainder of my walk, I pronounced that the blood of Jesus was over my family, our home, Jim's job, and all that touched our lives. When I returned from my walk, Jim, who had an office in our home, informed me that he just received a phone call and was to report to the main headquarters in two days.

In my husband's line of work, he was considered a road warrior. He maintained an office in our home and traveled extensively throughout the Midwest for the paper industry. His company's headquarters were in Pennsylvania, and the phone call said for him to report there posthaste. Jim was concerned about the immediateness of the trip, especially because they gave no reason other than to just be there quickly. The paper industry was struggling to maintain their piece of the economic pie. Many facilities had been shut down with no warning, but we agreed that God would take care of us regardless of how we felt. I flippantly said, "They aren't going to put out all this money for planes, trains, and automobiles and then fire everyone when they could avoid the expense with just a phone call." So we continued to do what we knew to do: pray and apply the blood of Jesus over the situation.

We have an enemy. His name is Lucifer, the devil, Satan, Beelzebub, or whatever you want to call him. He is a devourer, and his favorite dish is fear. He will whisper lies and try to get you to feel the fear and believe all is lost. He whispered in my ear and tried to get me to believe "Jim is going to lose his job." The devil was looking for the aroma of fresh meat. But even though the enemy roared with his lies, we chose to believe God's word that says, "A thousand may fall at your side, and ten thousand at your right hand, but it shall not come near you" (Ps. 91:7, TAB).

Two days later, Jim called from the headquarters in Pennsylvania. He had just gotten out of his high-level meeting. *Jesus, I trust you,* was all I could breathe. Jim's voice was clear, but constricted. I could sense he was upset. He said, "Eight people were called into the meeting today, seven were let go." A pause, and then he said, "I still have a job." Jim was the only one retained that day. The lions had roared with their lies, but the word of God and the blood of Jesus had not lost its power. This was the beginning of a very long journey of learning and leaning on God's promises—the word of God—listening to his still small voice, and fine-tuning our ears to his frequency alone while the low roar of young lions circle their prey.

Know Who You Are in Christ

In order to hear the voice of God, you must first know who you are in Christ. Most of us go through our lives living and praying that everything will work out in the end, just hoping for the best. Do you know in your heart, if you laid your head upon your pillow tonight and you slipped into eternity, where you would go? Do you have the assurance deep down inside of your soul that you would be standing in the presence of an Almighty God, wrapped in the loving arms of your Savior, Jesus the Christ? Or do you have the fear of hell, fire, and brimstone? We all live forever and have a choice as to where that forever will be.

To make sure you know where you are going, there is no time like the present to settle the matter. I would be remiss in going further without giving you an opportunity to make things right with God. If you have any concerns about your eternity, on the back page of this book there is a prayer just between you and God to help get things straight. I'll wait for you.

So knowing who you are in Christ means that you have accepted God's love and agree with what he has said about you. "In Christ" means you are now a joint heir to everything that God has through Jesus, the Son of God. You are not a distant cousin but God's child. You are *in Christ* and are eligible to all the benefits of being a child of God. Those benefits include life eternal, healing, prosperity, freedom, wisdom, and a peace that goes beyond understanding. However, Jesus did not die just so that we could live a life unto ourselves. He died so that we would not have to live a life away from him.

When Jesus becomes your Savior, he also needs to become your Lord. Either he is Lord of all, or not Lord at all. This is key to hearing God's voice: laying down your life because Jesus laid down his life for you. Many do not want to go this far with their relationship with the Lord. They enjoy the long-distance connection like old friends, visiting him on their timetable, not his.

God wants the very best for us, and we would be shortsighted if we do not seek his perspective. Do you know the Lord knows your end from the beginning? There is a plan and purpose for your life. His Word says, "For I know the thoughts and plans that I have for you, says the Lord, thoughts and plans for welfare and peace, and not for evil, to give you hope in your final outcome" (Jer. 29:11, TAB).

However, the beautiful thing about laying down your life for him is he will give it back to you, and it will be better than you could have ever imagined. You see, our Heavenly Father not only loves us, but he wants us to be blessed. Then, in turn, we will be able to bless others. He wants us to have hopes, dreams, and even possessions.

The only stipulation is those things must not *have* us. "I came that they may have and enjoy life, and have it in abundance (to the full, till it overflows)" (John 10:10, TAB). However, he is a jealous God, so be sure to keep a For Sale sign handy, just in case your priorities get mixed up and you need to let go of whatever is between you and your relationship with the Lord.

So back to the story. The company Jim worked for was going through downsizing like a lot of corporations. He had been with them over ten years. We watched the paper industry in West Michigan begin to fade like a well-worn piece of fabric. Paper mills were closing, and jobs were disappearing. We lived in Michigan most of our married lives, and Jim had always worked in the paper-manufacturing industry. Our families, church, and lives were all in Michigan. I worked most of our married life, and I always tried to work within an educational system or company that would let me have school hours. I felt it was very important to be home when my boys were home. The Bible says, "A child left to himself brings shame to his mother" (Prov. 29:15, NKJV). Boy, isn't that the truth! Our sons, Ryan and Matt, were great kids; but they were boys, and they could find things to get into even if I *was* at home. However, at this particular time in my life, the boys were in college, and I had just quit one of the greatest jobs I'd ever had. I was a front office high school secretary, but my time of grace to work at that hectic level was over, and I found myself going through a bit of an identity crisis. I was tired, and I was right smack in the middle of menopause. So I thought it would be good to take some time off to find myself and regroup a bit.

Hearing God's voice is often in hindsight. I remember one of the first times I recognized his voice. My boys were young, around six and nine years old, and it had been a long day for me. Jim must have been traveling because I cooked macaroni and cheese for dinner, which we normally did not have when Jim was home. Wives of traveling husbands know the routine. You go right to the easy comfort food when you don't have to cook for the hubby. So the boys were eating—or should I say *not* eating at the dining room table. They were being kids and goofing around, and it was beginning to really annoy me. I remembered moving from the kitchen to the dining room with the thought I was going to let them have a taste of my irritation. As I came around behind them, still somewhat out of sight, I could literally feel this hump rising up on my shoulder, my arms reaching to the floor, and my fingernails growing at a scary, clawlike rate. My teeth morphed into fangs, and as I slithered around the corner assuming the position to devour the children, I heard a voice behind me say, "Chocolate." That one word stopped me in my tracks. I paused and turned back to the kitchen with my hump deflating and my arms, fangs, and nails returning to normal as I slunk back into the kitchen like a dried-up old prune. I realized I had only heard one word, but that word saved my children that day. You see, twenty minutes prior to this event, I had eaten a chocolate bar and washed it down with a caffeinated beverage. That combination of sugar and caffeine totally changed my demeanor from a loving mother with the patience of a saint to that ugly old troll who wanted to devour her children, just because they were messing around with their macaroni and cheese.

The Lord has a great sense of humor, and, fortunately for my kids, so did I. He has shown me many times after the "chocolate" incident that one word spoken by God can change the course of my life. I slowly learned to listen to the God that knows me better than I know myself, and also to stay away from the chocolate-caffeine combo. So when I heard the words, "Fear not," while taking my walk that day, I knew there was something coming up that I'd better not fear and pay attention to it, and it wasn't chocolate!

The only way I know to not have fear is to have faith in its place. Fear and faith do not mix, like oil and water. For example, when your daddy tells you to jump off the porch and he will be right there to catch you, you trust him, don't you? With wild abandon, you jump off into his waiting arms, knowing that he will be there for you. God said in my heart, "Fear not. Just jump. I will catch you." I made a decision that day to trust his loving arms, and I jumped off into the fearless unknown.

In hindsight, when I gave my heart to the Lord all those years ago on Christmas Eve, I knew Christ died for me, and my sins were forever forgiven. But even though Jesus was my Savior at that time, I did not know God as my Father. How many of us know that we are saved and heaven is ours but we do not have that kingdom living and lifestyle that the Bible promises? Jim and I were entering into a journey that would teach us about trusting God as our Father and finding the kingdom of God right in our own hearts.

Hindsight Diary 1

Know Who You Are in Christ

This is your opportunity to either write in a journal or make this your own hindsight diary. Write down who you believe you are "in Christ." Then write about the first time you *think* you heard God's voice. Relax and allow yourself to be like a little child hearing your father's voice for the first time.

Obedience Is Better than Sacrifice: The First Downsizing

Eight were called in, only one remained. We were very sad for those let go that day, but we were so thankful to be spared. Jim's position would now change. In this experiment, as they called it, he would be repositioned, have a new boss, and would go back to working on product development that he worked on ten years before. He would still be out in the field but with a different title, no company car, more work, same pay. You know the deal—getting more for less. We were grateful but not quite sure where this was leading. We knew we had been spared for a purpose and made the decision to be thankful and trust God. The scripture says, "Lean on, trust in, and be confident in the Lord with all your heart and mind and do not rely on your own insight or understanding. In all your ways know, recognize, and acknowledge Him, and He will direct and make straight and plain your paths" (Prov. 3:5–6, TAB). We chose to trust him, and even though we did not understand all that was happening to us, we knew the word of God was true, and God says, "Behold, to obey is better than sacrifice" (1 Sam. 15:22, TAB).

We were thankful that we could stay in West Michigan but sensed that this might be a mixed blessing. Time passed, and it began to feel like our own Egypt experience, as with the Israelites, slaving for Pharaoh making bricks with straw. We found out quickly that Jim's new boss was a micromanager and very demanding and critical. It profoundly affected him. He had always been praised for his work and admired, but now Jim slowly began to sink into despair. Many times, he said that he felt he was at the bottom of a well and could not get out. He physically had become out of sight and out of mind. And worse yet, when he prayed, all he heard from God was the word *persevere*. The favor seemed to fall off our lives like the colored leaves dropping from the maple trees during the autumn months in Michigan. We had always been the couple that seemed to have everything together. We had a nice home, great kids, and a very positive and upbeat attitude toward life. However, something shifted in our lives, and we began to spiral downward. Trusting God was not as easy as it use to be. You know, it's always easier to trust the Lord when you have money in your bank account and things are going well. What choice did we have anyway? Bag it now, curse God, and die? No, this was the time to walk the talk. Letting our faith have feet. We chose to believe in God's promises that said, "We are assured and know that [God being a partner in their labor] all things work together and are [fitting into a plan] for good to and for those who love God and are called according to [His] design and purpose" (Rom. 8:28, TAB). But what was the plan?

During this time of Jim's job issues, the foundation of our home began to crumble as well. My identity was illusive, my insides were in torment, and you know the saying, "If Momma ain't happy, ain't nobody happy." The doctors said I was in full-blown menopause, but the good news was I would be finished by the time most of my lady friends would have just started. Well, they were wrong. That ordeal lasted ten long, hot, frustrating years. Anyone who has faced down the eye of that storm will confirm that it is a nightmare. Unfortunately, I didn't know much about menopause, nor did I look for the help I needed to fight the curse until almost too late. This was not just menopause; this was earth-moving, fire-spitting, volcanic meltdowns. One moment I was Cindy the Saint, the next moment I turned into Hurricane Cindy—and boy could I blow up a storm! The hot flashes were spontaneous and the reaction to them just as bad. Mood swings, tears, confusion, brain fog, and night sweats just to name a few. The doctors just kept putting me on pills, patches, and downers. I literally had to fight every step of the way to not lose my mind while at the same time trying to be supportive of my husband, be a good mother, and of course maintaining appearances. Jim admittedly said when I needed his help and support that he had nothing to give me. *Well, isn't that just great. Here I am being so saintly, and I had to go it alone?* (That was the menopause speaking.) So it was just me and God wrestling it out. Jacob did that in the Bible and said he would not let go until he got his blessing. Well, that was the path I chose to take. I would hang on to the Lord and say, "I will not let you go, God, until I get my blessing."

Life is a series of choices, good and bad. I had made a good choice. I was going to hang on and ride out this storm. Those who knew us had no idea what we were going through. We chose to fight this battle behind closed doors, and fight we did. We are told to fight the good fight of faith, but sometimes we fight with each other instead. Thank God for a good sense of humor; it got us through many a tense moment.

During one of those moments, my hormones decided to show up big time. I was trying to make a decision on what to wear for the day. Let me preface this story with an exclusion. I was not in my right mind. I don't know where it went, but it was gone nonetheless and left me to my own devices; Jim unfortunately took the brunt of it.

You're familiar with the scenario, ladies. You put on an outfit, and you ask your spouse how you look. Jim was trying to get into the shower, and I was insistent on having his opinion on the outfit immediately. He took a quick look and said, "It looks fine." Well, that was not the response I was looking for. He did not really even look at me. This was where the right side of my brain left. I actually saw it leave. *Whoosh*—right out the open window. Then I accused him of lying to me and not even looking just because he wanted to get into the shower. Now, my husband is the sweetest man on the face of this earth and did not deserve the wrath that was to come. If only I could have found the right side of my brain at that time, but it was off on some trip to insanity and left no forwarding address. So I ripped off the outfit, threw it on the bed, and put on another. Jim had not gotten into the shower yet, so I asked him his opinion on the next outfit. He looked and said, "That one is fine too." Then without notice or hesitation, my left brain exited off the trolley to join my right brain in the land of wherever. "Liar, why are you lying to me? Just tell me the truth," I said. Jim's face started to twitch in frustration. Again, I threw the outfit on the bed, muttering how could I have married such a liar and that God would surely strike him dead if he lied one more time to this saint. Yeah, right! The poor man was just trying to get into the shower, and I was determined to ruin his day and mine too. Another outfit was put on in haste. As I stood in front of the mirror, I said again, "How does this look?" Again, his reply was, "Okay." Well, there was no winning to this. I stood there with no brain at all by now, literally just a talking head, and said, "Why don't you just tell me the truth?" Then the man I love more than life itself came totally unglued. Imagine that! Now I had done it. He slammed the door of the bathroom not once, not twice, but three times in his exasperation and said, "Who is this person and what have you done with my wife?" You know, there is just something funny about someone else losing their mind. *Slam, slam, slam* went the door, the veins on his neck were bulging, and his eyes bugging out. There he was in his altogether slamming the door not once but three times. Now that was funny!

I began to laugh, and laughed some more. It was one of the funniest things I think I had ever seen. In an instant, my right and left brain both joined in the laughter, and sanity snapped back into focus. I put on the outfit I had originally planned to wear in the first place, walked into the bathroom (Jim had finally made it into the shower—a cold one, I bet), and asked, "How does this look?" one last time. Jim cautiously opened the shower door, and said in a calm voice, "I'm not going there," closed the door, and continued on with his long, much-deserved shower. He was the saint, not me! Menopause, it is a curse!

Humor is a great diffuser. We can get so wrapped up in stupid things and miss how funny the whole situation can be. We take life and ourselves far too seriously. I was going to need this sense of humor during this next season. Passing through menopause was by far one of the worst experiences in my life. Most of it was needless suffering. It's chemistry, not the devil. We give the devil access in our lives through sin, but menopause has to do with a change in life, one that we women don't ask for but get anyway. The way we handle that change can not only affect our lives but those around us. The Bible says in Proverbs 10:14, "Wise people store up knowledge." It is important to get knowledge, then wisdom comes alongside to guide and direct you. I did not have the knowledge of what to do about menopause, and it affected my life, my tongue, and my actions more than it ever should have. A valuable lesson learned. Ladies, have your hormones checked. You must take good care of yourself. What you do now affects you for a lifetime. We are only given one earth suit while on this planet. It is our responsibility to take care of it. Do your due diligence; you owe it to yourself, your family, and your God!

Hindsight Diary 2

Obedience Is Better than Sacrifice

The Lord does not want your sacrifice; Jesus already gave his life for you, but he does require obedience. Obedience, simply put, is to trust the one who gives the orders. We are to trust the Lord and roll our works and problems over to him and just obey, plain and simple. Write about your struggles in trusting God. Divide those struggles into categories then find corresponding scriptures to help you overcome your lack of trust by replacing those fears with what God's word says about it.

Lack of Vision

Shortly after what we affectionately called the "clothing incident," our pastor preached on lack of vision. He taught, "If you do not have vision for your life, get under someone else's vision and you will find yours." That phrase turned over in my mind like an old butter churn, cranking the wheel to turn cream into butter. *Get under someone else's vision to get yours.* He was reading my mail. I had no vision at all. I felt I had no direction and no identity. I did not know which way to go and apparently couldn't even figure out the simplest task of getting dressed, plus Jim had lost his vision too. He was just into maintaining and persevering.

During this time, our youngest son graduated from college and was living with us. He was having a difficult time finding a job, so his vision wasn't clear either. We were all pretty much floating adrift. Now, you must understand, this is a family who looks from the outside to have their act totally put together. However, we, like so many others—maybe even you—have put on a great façade. Oh, if only they knew; but if they really did know what was going on, would they think less of us? Or even worse, have pity on us? Heaven forbid. We will just keep these trials to ourselves. We should have sought guidance, wisdom, and counsel, but thank goodness for God's perfect timing.

I took a trip northward to visit my mother and found the help I needed in a Bible study that she attended. It changed the course of my life. You have heard the expression "being in the right place at the right time"? Well, this was one of those right places, and the timing could not have been better. There were two women at that Bible study who planted seeds in my very hormonal and visionless soul. One lady, Nan, was familiar with the church I was attending downstate and recommended a person for me to contact regarding serving in the church to get under someone's vision. The other gal, Joann, was an RN and recognized I was in extreme hormonal imbalance and recommended a natural progesterone cream for my menopausal meltdowns. She said my estrogen was very high and my progesterone very low, so I was totally out of balance. I can truly say that was one of my better days: two answers for the price of one.

You know, it is all well and good to get advice, but the most important thing about advice is to take it. As soon as I got home, I made an appointment with the person who was recommended to me at church to find a place to serve and find vision, and I also started looking for the natural progesterone cream to help with my out-of-balance hormones. I found the cream (or should I say it found me), and within five months, my mental and physical health improved 100 percent. It took ten years to get out of balance, so five months was worth the wait. My life was changing like a captain trimming the sails and setting course for some new land. The land of purpose, vision, and cooler waters was just around the corner.

Hindsight Diary 3

Lack of Vision

The Lord says that his own children perish and cast off restraint without vision. If you do not have vision for your life, it might be helpful to get under someone else's vision to help you find yours. Write down some things that you deeply care about then set a plan to either find someone else who cares about the same things to help you get started, or draft a plan for yourself.

It Is in Serving

Living as a Christian is not about me and you, it's about him, Jesus Christ. So how do we become God-focused and not self-focused? God's word says, "For whoever desires to save his life will lose it, but whoever loses his life for My sake will find it" (Matt. 16:25, NKJV). So I called and made an appointment with the ministry director for the television program our church produces. They broadcast a half-hour weekly program throughout the United States and across many nations. Their prayer-partner ministry is always on the lookout for those who have a heart to pray when the viewers call their prayer line. My meeting with the director, Deb, went very well, and we immediately struck up a friendship. We decided that I should come and sit with the prayer partners, listen to them taking calls, and pray to see if this was part of God's plan for my life. I've always been a person of prayer ever since I accepted Christ's salvation for me, and I loved to pray with and for others. I thought I would be well qualified for this task. But as I sat next to these saints of God behind walls where no one could see them, I saw faith in action. These wonderful warriors were laying down their lives, fighting in the trenches of spiritual warfare, and believing and standing on the word of God for people they did not even know and could not see. *Lord, how arrogant of me to think I could even do this,* I thought. But I knew that God had orchestrated this connection, so I decided to press through my doubts. After my three required visits sitting with the prayer partners, it was now my turn to be on the phone lines. We had a handbook with topics and scriptures to help us if we got stuck. I knew the Lord would direct the phone calls to the right person, and I prayed he would give me the words to speak to these precious callers. We did not counsel, we only gave the counsel of God's word.

I always tried to remind the callers when they wanted to tell me everything that was going on in their lives that they did not call to talk to me but to hear from God. "So let's talk to him together," I would say. I would also remind them we need to speak *to* the mountain, not about it. God's Word says, "For where two or three are gathered together in My name, I am there in the midst of them" (Matt. 18:20, NKJV). I wanted to hear the Lord speak to those precious saints. As we prayed and agreed together, through the tears on the other side of the phone, we felt the assurance that the Lord heard our prayers and his answer was on the way. It was not me but the word of the Lord that touched their hearts. My years on the prayer lines taught me to trust God's word and listen to his voice more than ever. He used this time to build my faith and to also teach me about obedience. There were many days I did not want to go to the ministry center and pray for others when I needed so much prayer for myself, Jim, and my family.

There were many days when I certainly did not feel like I had any answers or scriptures for those precious people that called. Then I would remember, it's not about me. I continued to trust him and be obedient, "and being fully convinced that what He had promised He was also able to perform" (Rom. 4:21, NKJV). This was God's call, not mine. The drive to church was thirty minutes one way, and I used that time to pray in the spirit and sing praises to the Lord. This did wonders for my day. Not only was I built up, but I also came into the ministry center ready to hit the ground running, laying aside any weight that would keep me from standing at my post.

One of those days serving in the television ministry happened on September 11, 2001 (9/11). It was my day to answer the phones in the prayer office. There was a telethon for our local TV station, so our program was not broadcast, but I decided to go in anyway in case there was a stray phone call and pray-over written requests that came through the mail. There were three of us in the prayer room that day, and like always we had the television on softly as we were reading our Bibles and praying scriptures over written requests. Then the news alert came across the screen. I imagine we all can remember where we were and what we were doing on that fateful day. The broadcast showed the first plane had already hit one of the Twin Towers, and the news crews were scrambling trying to make sense of what was happening. The three of us—Sharon, Donna, and myself—began to pray earnestly for all involved. We were as much in shock as our whole country and did only what we knew to do. Then Donna, who was always quite prophetic, said, "Keep praying, there is another one." Just then we looked up at the screen and watched in horror as the second plane screamed through the second of the Twin Towers. We fell to our knees praying for those in the building, asking for God's intervention and mercy. "Lord, please help them," was our cry. We remained in the prayer room for several minutes, praying, then called our own families to make sure they were all okay. They were all watching in horror as we were, and we all decided we should be with our families now, especially not knowing what might happen next. By that time, all air traffic had been stopped, and people were sent home from their jobs and shopping as well. There was very little traffic on the roads on which was normally a very busy day. Everyone was glued to their television sets, watching in horror, wondering if this was the end of all things normal. I was several blocks from home when I decided I had better get some gas for the car. I was surprised to see at least twenty others waiting in line at the gas station as well. It was like a scene out of a disaster movie—people gassing up their vehicles before an alien invasion. That day changed the direction of the country, but it also changed the direction of our lives. I was so thankful to have been at my post, praying for our nation that day.

As Jim and I worked through this next chapter of our lives, we began to realize that we had our priorities mixed up. We were good churchgoing folks and believed and practiced tithing, I was serving in the television ministry, and Jim and I were both singing in the choir; but we were still not seeing the over and above blessed lifestyle—the pressed-down, overflowing life that Malachi 3:10 promised: "Bring all the tithes into the storehouse, that there may be food in My house, and try Me now in this," says the lord of hosts, " If I will not open for you the windows of heaven and pour out for you such blessing that there will not be room enough to receive it." *Where are those overflowing blessings in our lives?* We were looking for that "such a blessing" because there were still more daily expenses at the end of our monthly paycheck.

As Jim and I chatted with each other while taking our noontime walk, we realized that we were spending way too much time and money fixing and working around our home. This house was a new build on speculation, but it had no lawn or landscaping and there were lots of oak trees. We were constantly working on clearing the land, planting bushes and flowers, even to the point of missing church and other opportunities for relaxation. We found great enjoyment working on the house, and we built up this beautiful piece of property from nothing. However, a scripture kept floating through my mind, "For where your treasure is, there your heart will be also" (Matt. 6:21, NKJV). Our home had become our treasure. Yes, it is good to maintain and to improve, but we were serving the homestead instead of it serving us. Matthew 6:19 says, "Do not lay up for yourselves treasures on earth, where moth and rust destroy and where thieves break in and steal; but lay up for yourselves treasures in heaven." Worse yet, all our hard labor was being thwarted by varmints. Everything we planted was like a lunch buffet set up for the rabbits, squirrels, raccoons, and moles. Those little thieves were devouring all our beautiful plantings. We tried everything to deter them from harvesting our lovely gardens. We even used cayenne pepper, but the rabbits brought out the little mariachi bands and had a festival! Jim and I decided God might be talking to us about our treasures, so we repented. Nothing can be more important than the call of God in our lives and serving him, not even this piece of property.

Hindsight Diary 4

It Is in Serving

Galatians 5 says that we are free in Christ, but we are not to use this freedom selfishly but to lovingly serve one another. It is in serving that we find ourselves. Have your priorities become a little upside down? This would be a great time to write down ways you can start serving in the local church or your community.

Repentance Precedes Deliverance

During this season, I was reading Haggai, the thirty-seventh book of the Bible. It speaks of a time to consider your ways. Sowing but not reaping, eating but never filled, earning wages and never gaining, like having a bag with a hole in it. That described our lives. We could never seem to get ahead. There was always something going wrong, demanding money and time. God's Word went on to say, "Is it time for you yourselves to dwell in your paneled houses while this house [of the Lord] lies in ruins?" (Hag. 1:4, TAB). I felt convicted. We had been spending so much of our time and money on a large house we no longer needed, with a debt too big to handle. I believed it was time to sell the house, downsize, and move closer to the church. It became more than just a thought; it was pure conviction. Jim was not as receptive to this idea as I was. We had spent a lot money and time getting the current house just the way we liked it. "You want to sell it and move to the other side of town?" Jim groaned. Then I gently reminded him of the treasure principle of "where your treasure is, there your heart will be also" (Luke 12:34, NKJV). I really believed that we had put far too much time and money into our current home. Jim didn't quite see us having to move to settle this treasure problem. However, little did we know there would be larger decisions coming our way that would require courage and wisdom that we may not have had if we kept our big house with a much larger mortgage. Again, God's timing is perfect. We just need to pray for wisdom and the courage to move when God says move or stand, and stay when he says to do so, listening to that still small voice of God, fine-tuning our hearing to his frequency. Jim and I agreed that if the Lord wanted us to move to the other side of town, he would show us. We knew the Lord would order our steps as we made our plans because Proverbs 16:9 says, "A man's heart plans his way, But the lord directs his steps" (NKJV). Or as Jim would say, "We have to give God something to work with, you have to be riding a bike to be able to turn it."

It was about that time the Lord started waking me up on a regular basis very early in the morning, 3:33 a.m. to be exact. I would just wake up, turn, and look at the clock, and it would be 3:33. I could hear the words in my favorite book of the Bible say, "Call to Me, and I will answer you, and show you great and mighty things, which you do not know" (Jer. 33:3, NKJV). I knew the Lord was calling me in the wee morning hours, just like Jeremiah, to spend time with him. My relationship with the Lord grew during those nighttime rendezvous, by me just listening and fine-tuning to his frequency. Again, it was obedience. I did have a choice whether to get up or not, drag myself out from the warm covers, place one foot in front of another, and plod to the sofa downstairs to kneel and pray and feel my Father's presence. I did not want to miss a thing the Lord would say to me. As I went to my knees and say, "Yes, Lord, your servant is listening," he would speak to my heart with these words, "What do you see?" I would look up or ahead at something, and the Lord would explain to me what I saw. Not in the natural, but beyond the veil of the natural. It would always be very simple, much like a parable. That was the way God spoke to my heart. I later learned as I studied more in the book of Jeremiah, the Lord spoke to that prophet of old in the same way: "The word of the lord came to me, saying, 'Jeremiah, what do you see?'" (Jer. 1:11, NKJV).

Hindsight Diary 5

Repentance Precedes Deliverance

We must walk with a penitent heart. We sin often and fall short of the glory of God. Write down what you think your limitations are and then write about God's unlimited power regarding your self-perceived limitations. Allow God to deliver you from the thoughts that hold you back from your deliverance.

Decision Comes before Vision

The Lord is faithful. He knows our frame and how much we can take. However, we have to follow the rules set up in his rule book. "Call upon me…he who dwells in the secret place…" These are commands that God gives, and if we follow them, the Lord says, "[Then] He will deliver you from the snare of the fowler and from the deadly pestilence. [Then] He will cover you with His pinions, and under His wings shall you trust and find refuge; His truth and His faithfulness are a shield and a buckler" (Ps 91:3–4, TAB). It seems like God always has a *then*—if you do this *then* I will do that!

These are God's promises and principles. I believed that God would confirm what I was supposed to do. I still struggled with purpose but trusted the Lord would direct my footsteps.

At that time, I was attending a women's ministry on a weekly basis. We could pick and choose different workshops every week, depending on the subject matter. I attended one particular study that was taught by the very woman who had directed me to the television ministry.

She, once again, had a significant word for me; I noticed this timing issue had become very important in hearing God's voice. She taught on the refiner's fire, a teaching I had not heard before. She got my attention and was defining my life perfectly. She asked, "Are you doing everything you know to do—tithing, serving, loving God and mankind—but still in turmoil, not feeling complete, knowing there is something more, but everything around you is falling apart or away?" *Yes*, was my internal response. "Struggling with who you are and why you are?" *Yes*, again. "Nothing is moving and everything is just seeming so pointless?" *Yes, yes, yes*. Then she said it: "Have you ever considered you might be in the refiner's fire?" It felt like someone just blew the cap off my head and slapped me backward. It was my aha moment. "You mean all this stuff that I'm going through—not knowing my purpose, and everything falling away and apart—was actually the fire of God burning off the dross in my life?" Then she said, "Have you ever said to God, 'I want all of you, and you take all of me, and whatever is not of you, Lord, just take it away"? *Oh yeah, I was in the refiner's fire all right!*

The fire of the Refiner is mentioned in Malachi 3. It's like this big boiling pot. You get put in a kettle and the heat is turned up. The things in your life that need to be discarded, that keep you from your purpose, are boiled away. With the heat, those things in your life that are not of God come loose and float to the top. Then the Refiner (God) skims the dross off the top and looks down to see if he can see his reflection. It's a process: boiling, straining, looking down, boiling, straining, looking down, until His reflection is clear. When I realized this was my life and I was in a very hot spot, I said in fear and trembling, "Turn up the heat, God!" I did not want to stay in the fire any longer, and the quickest way to get out of the pot was to turn the heat up. Within two weeks, I was out of the pot, and clarity was coming.

During this time, Jim and I believed that I should still work, but I now wanted to work in the church. Ever since I was born again, I believed I was to work in the ministry in some form or fashion. Now it was time to acknowledge what I felt was the Levitical call on my life, which is to work within the walls and covering of the church. Let me tell you that right from the start, it must truly be a call from God to work for the church. Just because you feel a call or a want to work in the church, it does not mean that it is always smooth sailing, or that it is right for you. However, the impression grew so strong that I decided to voice my belief to those I trusted in the television ministry and see what counsel they would give me. Thus came another turn in my life. When I mentioned my desire to no longer work in the secular world, the director of the television/prayer ministry literally flew out of her office at my announcement and said, "If you are really serious about working for the church, go right now and fill out an application at the main desk. Nobody gets a job here without filling out an application first." She marched me down to the front office and introduced me to the head receptionist, who was the keeper of the applications. We had no idea if there were actually any open positions available; we just knew an application needed to be filled out to land a job at this church. Two days later, while attending the women's ministry meeting, Deb approached me and said the office manager / pastor's assistant was asking about me and wanted a recommendation. Within two hours, I had my one and only interview, and was hired the following Saturday. I was offered a position in the reception area. My head was spinning so fast that I neglected to ask what my position required me to do. I chose to trust that this was the Lord's doing and followed his lead. I knew this was an answer to prayer and God would provide details later.

When I showed up for work, I was surprised that my new assignment at the church was to be placed behind a six-foot wall to answer the switchboard at half the pay I was used to making! I had another choice to make right then and there: follow God, trusting that he is my promoter, or flee in hurt and rejection. Since following God has always worked before, I guess I needed to stick around and see what he had in mind for me.

My first day was a whirlwind. I was suppose to be trained by the head receptionist, but she was called away from her desk within ten minutes of my arrival, and I was left on my own to steer this massive boat of a church with a congregation approaching seven thousand. The phones were ringing, and people were at the desk looking for answers. All I can say is when the Lord takes you to something, he always gives you what you need to go through it. I put a demand on the grace of God, and he brought up all of my resources and experiences from my past work and the ship stayed on its course. When the receptionist returned, she was very apologetic for leaving me but tremendously relieved that I was able to hold the helm. All the while, I was wondering why God had taken me back so far that it felt I was starting all over again. He spoke to my heart and said this was just a "springboard" experience. He explained to me that as you dive into a pool from the diving board, to get the greatest lift, you should step back to get the momentum to go forward for the big jump. I had no idea that there would be another big jump coming up.

God was showing us that my new position at church was the first step for Jim and me to move forward on selling our home and continuing on our right track. We now needed to find a house that was suitable in size, mortgage, and location near the church. We looked at preexisting homes, but nothing felt right. We believed the Lord might have another option that we had not considered. Then I heard an ad on the Christian radio station of a builder whose slogan was, "Building on a firm foundation." I decided to stop by their model home to check them out. Within moments, I knew they were the ones that would help us to fulfill this part of our journey. We would downsize, build a smaller home that would be easier to maintain and afford, and keep our priorities straight.

The process of building a home can be quite tedious, but with the Lord, it is amazing how the peace that goes beyond understanding will undergird everything around you. This particular builder just happened to have a development within one mile of the church and absolutely the best shopping and restaurants in West Michigan. All we had to do was choose the lot and the style of home. We planned for this to be our last house for quite a while. We called it our *retirement home.*

We really liked one particular ranch design they had, but it was a little short on square footage. Our budget was tight, and we were downsizing in money as well as keeping our treasures in the things not of this world. After looking at many options, Jim and I decided to look at one particular model home one more time. Interestingly, on that day, a different salesperson *just* happened to be showing the home and mentioned that this particular model was on sale, dropping the price by nine thousand dollars if we broke ground before winter. That drop in price would allow us to add and afford the extra square footage we needed without the extra cost. Talk about being in the right place at the right time. God was directing our steps just like he said he would. It is so important to mention here that we were just trying to follow the Lord's leading, listening to that still small voice, and following the open doors. The world is loud and always in a hurry. We must quiet our soul, our emotions, our flesh, and our worries and trust that the Lord will direct us. It is that still small voice that you need to listen to. The book of Isaiah says, "Your ears will hear a word behind you, saying, This is the way; walk in it, when you turn to the right hand and when you turn to the left" (30:21, TAB). After deciding the style and size of our new home, choosing the lot was much easier. Often, that is the progression of faith, taking life one step at a time. It seems like God never reveals his whole plan to us in the beginning. I think that's because if we were to know the whole thing, we would go out and try to fulfill it ourselves, not fully knowing God's purpose and all the steps and stops that need to occur along the way. It is precept upon precept, line upon line, one thing at a time. God knew our future and the outcome and all the bumps coming up in our journey that we would have never withstood had we not downsized our home and the mortgage.

We were able to break ground before winter set in and began to prepare our current home to sell. Jim and I could feel change in the wind. Not just in the physical but in our spirit, we could feel the Lord doing a new thing. The next five months flew by. Jim was still struggling with his job. His boss was more demanding than ever, the company was floundering in the industry, and the future in the natural looked a little shaky, but we pressed on because we knew God was ordering our steps. Designing and working together on our new home was a time of goal-setting and planning for our future. We had an underlying assurance that God was directing us, and we knew he had a plan for our lives.

Within six weeks of working behind the six-foot wall in the front office of the church, answering the switchboard at half the pay and twice the work, I was promoted to the head receptionist position with responsibility over five part-time receptionists and a pay increase to match that level of authority. The current head receptionist, after fourteen years and many attempts from other ministries to pry her from her post, accepted a position in the women's ministry, which allowed for the door to open for my promotion. We had wonderful chats together, acknowledging God's marvelous timing and his order of doing things. She slipped into her new position and blossomed and grew in her gifts to the glory of God. It was my honor to be given the head receptionist position and to steer the front desk and guard the leadership of my church during that time. I had to step back on the diving board to get the momentum to go forward. Promotion does come from the Lord in *his* timing.

While our house was being built, there were many decisions that had to be made on a daily basis. We decided to sell our current home on our own, wanting to capture as much money as possible. However, we did interview some professionals, but their grasp of our reality was different in timing and price. We've used realtors in the past, and I also worked for one long ago, so we felt confident that we could do a FSBO (for sale by owner) this time. Our new home would be completed in five months. Jim and I made a large professional sign and took great care to place it strategically so all could see it on a near by corner. After several months a woman traveling on her way to work decided to go a different route. She saw our sign and called. We chatted for more than an hour on the phone. She seemed to be more interested in our lives than in the house. She asked a lot of personal questions that a casual looker normally would not. We had a great conversation, and it was almost an afterthought for her to come and look at the house. We agreed that she and her husband would come by that Sunday after church. As usual, Jim and I were outside working on the yard when they drove up. They had their little boy with them, and he jumped out of the car and proceeded to thoroughly enjoy himself running through the woods playing in our very secluded backyard. We chatted outside with the husband and wife while their little boy was in his own world of cowboys and Indians on the trail of some wild beast. We finally went inside after almost an hour and took a brief tour of the house. We shared our story of how we believed we were to move closer to our church and that were only stewards of this lovely home. Jim and I felt we very well may have been preparing this home for someone else then they said they believed they were that someone else! An offer was received from them that night with no contingencies on selling their current home. They truly believed if this was the Lord, he would sell their house too; and he did, one week before we signed the closing papers, April 24, exactly five months to the day that our new home was completed. I've noticed the Lord has lots of opportunities to be early, but he is never late. His timing builds our faith and character, and he works in such a way that he alone gets the glory.

I want to stop here and say that just because we believed we were in God's will doesn't mean this was not a struggle. We did go through some stuff along the way. But the bottom line is God is faithful, and he will direct your paths. However, you must be in a place in your heart where you are willing to lay things down and trust him. This is not easy; that's why they call it a battle. You wrestle with your will, you wrestle with the enemy of your soul, and you wrestle with the Lord. You may even wrestle with the ones that are closest to you. But the battle belongs to the Lord, and the victory is ours. God was developing us, maturing our walk, and strengthening our faith so that we could stand when the winds of doubt and fear would roar. God's word is a sure foundation; you can stand on it. These struggles and victories were but a training period for us. We were learning to capture our thoughts and submit them to the word of God. We used God's word as our filter. If our thoughts and actions did not line up with God's word, then we had to adjust *our* thinking. This was new for us. Jim and I found we tend to adjust our thinking to how we are feeling. Feelings can mislead us and are based only on the moment. God's word is true and eternal. However, you must have God's word in your heart to be able to use it as a filter; and that would, of course, require reading it. Jim and I made an effort to read God's Word and speak his promises daily. This season was only preparation for a greater battle that was just around the corner. The enemy was just throwing small hand grenades our way this time; he had not begun the full assault.

Moving is always a challenge. Jim hates it. He has a better memory than I have when it comes to the amount of work it takes to accomplish a task. I, on the other hand, can see the completed project and focus so much on the finish line that I sometimes forget about what it takes to get to the end. Well, this was a bigger move than we had thought. Our younger son decided to move with us, which wasn't in the original plan. He was to be out on his own by now, but due to uncertainty in his employment, we believed it would be better for him to move with us,which meant more stuff to pack, move, and unpack. Plus, we had not planned on a bedroom for him, so he got the garden-level apartment—the unfinished basement. And unfortunately, I did not get a chance to sort through all our stuff before packing, so we ended up moving with it. We downsized in house, but not the crap.

We found we could not do this move on our own this time, so we hired some help. Plus, I promised Jim on the last move that if we moved again, we would hire professionals with strong backs. However, these movers also underestimated the amount of stuff we had and were not prepared either. For some reason, they didn't allow enough time to do the job well and rushed with our precious belongings—they were paid by the hour, so go figure—and we had damage. Not just damage to our possessions, but these "professionals" had damage to themselves as well.

I remember mentioning to the movers several times that the sofa bed on the second floor was very heavy, and we had to take it apart when we moved it up there in the first place. But they would have none of my advice. When I heard the crash and the yell for help, I knew we had trouble. By the time I arrived on the scene, some of my worst fears were staring at me. There were three men up above the sofa on the second-floor landing, and one man lay trapped underneath the sofa, holding it up with one hand and grasping the back of his neck with the other. I ran to him and bolstered up the sofa with all my might as the young man slowly slid down the rest of the stairs. The other two movers who were out in the garage heard my cry for help, ran in, and held the sofa so that I could assist the crumpled mover on my stairway. I was very concerned that he had damaged his neck, so I took great care in keeping him stable. Fortunately, we had wood floors at the bottom of the stairway, so I had him lie flat and was able to slide him over into the dining area, out of the way of the descending sofa, all the while praying loudly, proclaiming there would be no calamity on my watch in this house. I'm sure I scared everyone, but we were in a spiritual battle. The past was hanging and holding on, and the enemy was roaring. I admit, I was so focused on what lay on the other side of this move that I was not prepared for this attack. The movers came early that morning and Jim and I were so involved that we missed our prayers that day. But God is faithful. Jim and I continued to pray over this young man spread out on our dining room floor. We believed and agreed that the Lord would heal him. He was upset, in pain, pale with tingling and numbness in his toes, and very, very scared. I asked his foreman if we should call for an ambulance, but they decided to wait a bit to see if he felt better. I think they delayed due to his lack of insurance.

His skin remained pale and clammy, and I was very concerned that he might be going into shock. Again, I commanded the enemy to leave him alone. Looking into the young man's eyes, I asked him if he was right with the Lord; he said that he had recently been going to church and was trying to get his life back together, and he also planned to marry the mother of his child soon. We both agreed that was a very good idea. Amazingly, this turn of events in his life really caused him to rethink and get right with God. After about thirty long minutes, he decided to try and sit up; the tingling had stopped, and he started feeling more stable. We helped him to the glider on the front porch, the only piece of furniture not packed. He and I sat out there another fifteen or so minutes while the other three movers carried on with their jobs. While sitting with him, we got to know each other better. I wanted to keep him talking to make sure he was all right. He asked me lots of questions about my prayer language and how I prayed. He said he had never heard anyone pray that way before. I can say without a doubt that young man's life was changed that moving day. He renewed his faith in the Lord, and he was healed miraculously by the power of God. I don't know if he would have come to this turning point any other way, but God is faithful. We believe Romans 8:28 is always in force: "And we know that all things work together for good to those who love God, to those who are the called according to His purpose" (NKJV).

Eleven long hours later, the last truck was unloaded; and we had one more serious injury involving blood and more prayer, but we were in our new downsized home with all of our stuff. We took our time unpacking as Jim and I hoped this would be our last house until retirement, and hopefully beyond that. We planned for the long run in this new downsized home, with upgrades on certain things such as door handles that latched instead of turned for the ease of carrying groceries in the house, keeping the living area on the main level, and other considerations for as we grew old together. Jim and I believed we were in God's will, and we could sense his peace. We missed many sunrises and sunsets in our previous home, but now we had them back as well as the moon and stars. Our new home was in the middle of an open field, and we loved it. Our previous home was buried among tons of oak trees and all their droppings, with wildlife that ate everything in sight. This subdivision had no trees, no leaves to rake, no varmints to chase, and hardly any neighbors yet. We planned our landscaping with the intent of perennial color and appeal all year long with low maintenance. What a wonderful feeling to get to what we were supposed to be doing: serving in the house of the Lord because our home was no longer our treasure. It was almost maintenance free and with a mortgage we could handle. The scripture that started this journey was in the book Haggai.

> Is it time for you yourselves to dwell in your paneled houses while this house [of the Lord] lies in ruins? Now therefore thus says the Lord of hosts: Consider your ways and set your mind on what has come to you. You have sown much, but you have reaped little; you eat, but you do not have enough; you drink, but you do not have your fill; you clothe yourselves, but no one is warm; he who earns wages has earned them to put them in a bag with holes in it. Thus says the Lord of host; Consider your ways (your previous and present conduct) and how you have fared. Go up to the hill country and bring lumber and rebuild [My] house and I will take pleasure in it and I will be glorified, says the Lord [by accepting it as done for my glory and by displaying my glory in it]. (Hag. 1:4–9, TAB)

We realized our old home had become too important to us. That is idolatry, plain and simple. The Lord will have no other gods before him. We decided to give up that weight that so easily beset us and lay down our lives to follow after the God who saved our very souls. By moving closer to the church, we could no longer use the excuse of living too far away to participate in the services. By downsizing in house and mortgage, we could now give out of our resources over and above the tithe and give of ourselves as well. In our new home, we would plant the landscape this time with the intent of doing it only once and not continually adding to it. Time was precious. Serving in the church became more important to us.

Our two boys were no longer boys but growing into wonderful Christian businessmen. Our youngest son, who moved with us, stayed longer than he had planned, but it worked out well. His commute to and from work was three hours round-trip, so the savings on rent helped with his gas and expenses. It was nice still having him around. Matt was very low maintenance; he came and went as he pleased and took care of his personal needs without our help. His humor and keen insight have always blessed us. Our oldest son, Ryan, and his wife, Rebekah, lived only fifteen minutes from us and trips to visit our first grandchild were made often. Life was just about perfect. I loved my position at church and I was treated very well. God's favor was present on our lives, and we enjoyed the fellowship of our friends at church and with the choir. Saturdays and Sundays were busy, as our church had multiple services, but that's the life we wanted. The church started a building campaign, and since there were no more holes in our bags, we were able to give to the building fund while paying off debt and still saving for retirement. We truly believed if we helped build God's house, he would help build ours. We were fulfilling the first chapter of Haggai. Life seemed complete.

Hindsight Diary 6

Decision Comes before Vision

Often God does not give you the whole picture ahead of time. It's usually one step at a time, with God putting ground under your feet with each step. You know what they say: feel the fear and do it anyway. God maintains what he ordains. Write in your diary something that you have wanted to do and what your first step would be.

The Only Constant in Life (Other than God) Is Change

I didn't know where the change was coming from or where it would take me, but I knew there was another change coming. I felt an undercurrent of something getting ready to move. I was happy with my position at work, and I felt very comfortable there. I made more friends than I ever felt possible, and I was on a first-name basis with the senior staff of this awesome church. However, I felt a shifting in my spirit, somewhat like the smell of rain before the clouds are even on the horizon.

My position at church was to field the calls and people who had appointments or other business with this large organization. Our church was not a church unto itself, but we were a mother church and had more than forty affiliates and churches that we started. This was a leadership church. There was always something going on: an event, conference, music concerts, etc. Life was never dull. In fact, it was exciting. But still, I had this knowing down in my knower that change was on its way again for me.

I am blessed with the talent of organization and administration. There is a part of me that loves to set things in order. Some are called to the marketplace and they let their light shine and are movers and shakers. Some are called to stay at home and raise up the next generation, and some have a Levitical call on their lives to serve in the house of God. We all have a call; you can run, but you cannot hide from it. It wakes you up in the middle of the night. It looks back at you when you look into the mirror. There is something more, and you know it. God says to "seek me and you will find me." So I began to seek him more and more. Sometimes we just talk and talk to God, and we forget to listen. *Blah, blah, blah*, or should I say, *baaa, baaa, baaa*, like the silly sheep that we are. So when do we finally shut up? When we are sleeping. The Lord will speak to us in dreams and visions if we will not hear him in our waking hours. So here comes my dream sequence, and the reason for the title of this book.

This dream was as vivid and clear as if I had seen it on a movie screen. I was in a large plain room with people sitting in rows of chairs. There was another room next door that was connected with a set of double doors that were open so you could see into the next room. That room had a conference table and rows of chairs too, with people sitting in them. I was standing in place next to my chair in the first room, and from the back of the room entered Deb. She walked past me and turned back and signaled for me to follow her to the room next door where the conference table was. I walked behind her. I looked at her with puzzlement as she took her seat at the conference table. I asked her why she wanted me to follow her into that room. She looked at me and said, "I thought I heard the lion's roar." In the stillness of the moment, I realized that I was inside a building on an animal compound, like one you might find in Africa, and in the background I could hear the low rumblings of young lions. Then I woke up.

Well, a dream like that sticks with you. As I went into work that morning, it remained on my mind. This was more than a dream. Through my mind's eye I could still see it, like an open vision of sorts. I was at work, doing my job, but I could still see the animal compound in my mind. I wondered what the lions' roar meant, and why did Deb tell me she thought she heard them?

As I worked at the front desk of our massive church, people would come and go all day long. My large desk was the gateway to the main office, which was the hub of our own little universe, and I was the gatekeeper. I had the power of the buzzer. One could not get back to the leadership staff unless I let them pass.

There were several other ministries located all over the church, but the main office lay behind me. Deb would pass by my post often. That morning would be different. I had to talk with her about the dream. Like clockwork, she passed by, said hi, and went to the door, but I did not go for the buzzer immediately. "Do you have minute, Deb? I have a quick question," I said. She was also my friend, so of course she had the time. I told her about my dream and my question regarding roaring lions. Deb does not have a poker face and pretty much wears her feelings on her sleeve, so I knew immediately something was up by her facial expression. She did not have the time to tell me everything, but she did ask if I was happy with my position at the church. That was not the answer I was expecting. Happy, yes; but as mentioned before, I felt there was a change in the wind. That was all that was said that morning. My question was not answered quite the way I had hoped. In fact, it only added more to the mix. I knew that God was about to show me something, but as always, it would be in his time. That time would be short.

Life is a series of changes. Just when you think you have it all figured out, here comes another bend in the road. That same day, our senior pastor's assistant and office manager, the person who initially hired and supervised me, asked if I was happy in my position, or if I would like another challenge. I tried to keep a poker face, but I knew something was up. So, truthfully, I said, "I'm always up for a challenge." I was then informed of the need for a new assistant for Deb; this caused me to immediately remember the dream and how Deb walked by and asked me to follow her into the other room. Wow! In the Bible, God always says to "go there, and I will bless you." Going there involves change; it involves taking a step. We shouldn't change just for the sake of change itself; nonetheless, change can be very good. A change of scenery can help on an off day. A change of pace can help you recover from a hectic lifestyle. But a change in occupations or vocations really needs to be divinely directed by God. The Bible says, "The steps of a good man are ordered by the lord" (Ps. 37:23). I believed God was directing and divinely ordering my steps. He was disturbing my comfort zone and showing me in my dream that change was coming so I could respond correctly.

Within two weeks, I had my replacement trained at the front reception desk, and I was in my new position as administrative assistant to the director of the television ministry. This was the most wonderful opportunity I had ever been given. It was a win-win for me. I was able to use my administrative skills and pray for others too. My new boss was not just my boss but also my friend. Now some will say this could be dangerous to a friendship, and they would be right. However, when you have Jesus as the center of your life, you can trust that he will continue to finish what he began. Deb allowed me to bloom under her authority. She pulled gifts and talents out of me that had lain dormant far too long. The position fit like a glove. I had waited a very long time for this.

Jim was working harder than ever trying to keep the fires lit in Michigan within the paper industry. There were paper mills closing all around us in West Michigan, which left industries that had been there for more than a century gutted, and their machinery was sold off piece by piece. Hundreds of good people let go and looking for work. Even the company Jim worked for laid off many just to keep a couple of steps ahead of the competition. If we could hang on for just a few more years, Jim could go out on his own if need be and do consulting work. A few more years with this company and we could take an early retirement with benefits, and he could even start a new career if he wanted. *Just six more years, Lord, we could pay off the house in record time and then retire and really serve you.* The only constant thing about life is—yep, change. The lions were waking up from their naps, and they were hungry.

By now, we had been in our newly built downsized home for seven months, and this was the first time we had money at the end of the month in a very long time. It was really nice to be able to plan a vacation other than staying with relatives and camping. We were dreaming again. It's been said that money isn't everything. Well, that's true, but it sure helps. We finally saved up enough to pay off our credit card. I could hardly wait to write the check and get that monkey off our back. Every time I'd sit down to pay bills, I'd bring up the credit card account and get ready to write the check, to pay in full. Then I'd get a caution in my spirit, *Not yet*. "But, Lord, I want to get out of debt, we have the money," I'd whisper. It would be a little tight for a while, but that debt would be paid in full. Still I heard, *Wait*, in my spirit. "Okay, one more month and I'll pay it off." A few days later, I was listening to a financial planner on the radio, and he was talking about always keeping a reserve in your account for the unknown; a two-month's safety net was recommended. This sounded like wisdom, and wouldn't you know, the amount we had in reserve was equal to that formula.

December 2, 2005, was my first anniversary working for the church. That date celebrated what I thought was the beginning of the last job I would ever have. We would continue to serve this body of believers and live and dwell in this land God had given us, close to our family, children, grandchildren, and friends.

Jim was off traveling again, back to the home office in Pennsylvania. He very seldom went to Pennsylvania anymore, but they had called a department meeting that day and asked all to come in. Jim was a little anxious and said it felt a lot like two years before when they let go of the seven, but I had no feelings of fear or trepidation, no urge to pray or to apply the blood of Jesus, although we continued to do that daily anyway. I felt nothing. I was confident that we were fulfilling God's plan right where we were, and the Lord was in charge; after all, we were playing according to his plan, not ours, abiding in the cleft of the rock, staying in the secret place of the most high. Or were we approaching the eye of the storm? The phone rang at work; it was Jim calling me. He had been called into a meeting that had a very familiar feel to it and was concerned that the slashing of the sword was coming. The staff in the ministry center prayed for us. The phone rang a half hour later. My husband's voice was slightly constricted, but there was such peace that came from him I hardly felt the cutting of the blade when he said, "I'm no longer employed." The blood began to run from my head, and I could not breathe. My heart was beating like the sound of a marching band, and all I could hear was a white noise in my ears. And I thought I heard the sound of roaring young lions. I could hear Jim speaking, but my mind was somewhere it had never been before. I could feel fear knocking at the door of my heart, and I was holding the key. I had a choice right then and there whether to turn the key and let the fear in. I tried to stay focused on what Jim was saying. I grabbed my pen and paper and started writing down his words.

"We have a six months' severance package and continued medical benefits for six months and good references, but it's over." They took his laptop computer and case, and he flew home that day with a plastic grocery bag of his personal office items and no job.

Hindsight Diary 7

The Only Constant in Life (Other than God) Is Change

Other than the word of God, you must expect change. Change stretches us and keeps us pliable. We need to be like clay, pliable in the Master's hand. We certainly do not want our pots to crack, do we? We can be so set in our ways that we may have to be broken before we can be used. Write about how the Lord has softened you so he can mold you into *his* image.

Let the Peace of God Rule Your Heart in Christ Jesus

Psalms 91:1 was in full force: "He who dwells in the secret place of the Most High shall remain stable and fixed under the shadow of the Almighty [Whose power no foe can withstand]" (TAB). Jim was not the only one who lost his job that day. Seventy other coworkers, including his boss, had been cut from the payroll. He said it looked like a war zone. There were people wondering and wandering around in a state of shell shock. Jim, however, felt a peace and calm that went beyond understanding. He found himself comforting others and getting as much information on what the next step was for him. He even found himself consoling the one who had to administer the blade in this bloody downsizing. It was a dark day for that company but a new day for Jim. He said it almost felt like a relief. *How could that be?* "Peace I leave with you, My peace I give to you; not as the world gives do I give to you. Let not your heart be troubled, neither let it be afraid" (John 14:27,

NKJV). Jim's secret place was God's peace; he was hidden in the cleft of the rock. We knew that as long as we stayed close to the Lord, we would be under his shadow. Jim's former company gave him a good severance package, and there was unemployment compensation, but we knew we needed to immediately scale back on everything, not knowing when another job would come to the Allen household again.

It now became clear why I did not feel right about paying off that credit card. We were going to need those two months of reserve. Thank goodness we sold our previous large home and scaled back. God was preparing us for this downsizing in advance in more ways than we knew, including my changing positions at work, which allowed me to have benefits if I needed them. The vision was beginning to play out right in front of us, and the lions were roaring!

I was confident Jim would be employed soon. I hoped we would be able to keep the severance package and pay off debt with it, and maybe even take a mini vacation. Jim had years of experience, respected in the paper industry, and God was in control. After a time, we believed this downsizing was a good thing. We had been taught to go where you are celebrated, not just tolerated, so we knew that Jim would be appreciated in his next place of employment. Our destiny is geographical, and this was a perfect time to believe God for all that and more. So what if we have been given lemons? Let's open up a stand, market it, and sell it—lemonade, that is!

Hindsight Diary 8

Let the Peace of God Rule Your Heart in Christ Jesus

The Lord will give you peace in the time of a storm. He did *not* promise that you would not have trials though; the rain falls on the just and the unjust. However, he did promise that he would be with you through the trials and you would be an overcomer! Write about the last time you had a peace that went beyond understanding in the midst of a trial.

Timing, Purpose, and Destiny

Jim wasted no time in looking for employment. We believed it would be good to keep the momentum up. Strike while the fire is hot, so to speak. The severance package included some helpful guidelines in handling the shock and pain of being downsized. Jim did his due diligence in studying all the literature he was given. He filed for unemployment and jumped through all the hoops that the government put in front of him to collect what funds we could. My employer was incredible and said they would help us out if we needed benefits when Jim's ran out. That was six months away though, and he would surely be employed before then. We were going to make it through this. We had some good leads right away. A university nearby was looking for a foundation director for their paper science department, and a competitor of his former company was looking for a sales representative. We did not sign the noncompete agreement part of the severance package yet, which meant Jim could take a job from a competitor. So things looked quite bright. This was not going to be a long process at all. I could hardly wait for the severance check. It was a fair chunk of change, and we could sock that away and pay off debt and have a vacation before Jim started working again. This was a time for us to be thankful, not remorseful.

Unfortunately, it seems December is a hard month to schedule interviews. The holidays are on everyone else's mind and not on interviewing. We were going to have to face this holiday with no job and very little under the Christmas tree. Fortunately, I had done advance Christmas shopping, so my grandson and children were taken care of ahead of time. Jim and I decided that we would wait until he had a job again before we exchanged gifts. That Christmas wasn't easy. Even though there were job possibilities out there, the mind plays awful tricks on you; and if you open the door to those tricks, it brings in all kinds of junk with it. Your mind becomes the enemy's playground, and he does not play fair, especially during the holidays.

We should have planned better; we knew the paper industry was slowly disappearing, but we thought with Jim's vast experience, he would continue to be of value, but no one is indispensable. You may think about it, but planning to lose your job or being downsized is not something you dwell on, especially when the company you work for is doing all right. However, when downsizing happens, fighting the bitterness and anger is a fight for your life. Jim was working at forgiving and not letting hurt feelings get the best of him. God's grace was there, but so was the enemy. We purposed to find the purpose in this. Delays came in the interviewing process; and when the interview finally came with the competitor, we had to face a possibility that we did not want to consider—moving to Vermont. We had just moved and felt we were where God wanted us to be. We were planted and happy, even in the midst of this storm; but this was a good job, and there were not many others out there.

The university position we heard about went on an indefinite hold, and then we heard the competitor decided to fill their position locally, so Vermont went off the radar. I was relieved that we didn't have to move, but now what? Okay, we still have the unemployment checks and the severance money, and we could sign the noncompete agreement, which meant a little extra money. The severance was good, but by the time the government was finished taking their part, it was only half the original amount. We knew we had to cut back on everything yet again, tightening up another notch on the belt, so to speak.

The Lord sustained us, but there was a battle going on in our minds. I fought my mind battles working in the ministry center while Jim was fighting his battles at home, alone in his home office. And we even fought some battles with each other now and again too. We had been married thirty-two years at that time and had never faced this kind of difficulty. Jim had always been occupied with a job and had focus. Now he was home all the time, focusing on getting a job and dwelling on the fact that he didn't have one. I had no idea of all the battles he went through, but he learned to wrestle with his God; and when you wrestle with the Lord, guess who always wins?

Timing is something that is hard to grasp; it is like trying to catch the wind. But the Lord's purposes are so far above ours, and when we allow him to work in our lives, he prevails in ways that we cannot. Sure, Jim could have gone out and gotten a job bagging groceries, but we knew the Lord was in control, and we did not feel a release for him to do anything but look for his new job. His full-time job was to get a full-time job. We believed that God meant what he said in his word which was, "Let the beauty of the lord our God be upon us, and establish the work of our hands for us; yes, establish the work of our hands" (Ps. 90:17, NKJV). It was God's will for Jim to work, and he will establish the work of his hands. Amen!

Hindsight Diary 9

Timing, Purpose, and Destiny

The first step to favor is being at the right place at the right time. This is done by steadily following the principles in God's Word. You do this, and he will do that. What was the last thing God told you to do? Write down what it was and if you completed the task. And if not, why?

Not Forsaking the Assembling of Ourselves

We could not fight this fight on our own. It was the Lord's battle for sure, and we could not carry this weight and fight the good fight without support from our family and friends. We were involved with our choir at church, and they were a tremendous support system, but Jim needed "man time." There was a great men's ministry that Jim had always wanted to be a part of, and now that his schedule had lightened up a bit, he had the time to finally get involved. I'm sure it was hard in the beginning for him. After all, a man's identity rests on what he does—his vocation, his position in life. When you introduce yourself, the next question is always, "What do you do?" Right there, you have a choice on what to say. We learned there is the truth and then there is the fact; we tend to get them confused. This is where Jim learned about the confession of his mouth. All the browbeatings I gave him at home on his words and nagging him about, "What is it you want to do?" never helped him as much as getting the word of God inside of him and confessing what God says about him. He learned this along with the other men at those early morning meetings. God has a purpose and a great plan for his life. The fact is, yes, he was unemployed; but the Word of God says to, "Roll your works upon the Lord [commit and trust them wholly to Him; He will cause your thoughts to become agreeable to His will, and] so shall your plans be established and succeed" (Prov. 16:3, TAB).

This was the first scripture Jim put to memory. These words changed from God's words of promise to God's personal prophecy to Jim. The change from doing it Jim's way to God's way started when the word became alive and dwelt in him.

Getting another job was taking far longer than we had expected. We had gone from three months to six months in a blink of an eye. There were very few prospects on the horizon, and those tiny specks of hope were in no big rush to interview. *What was God waiting for? How would God get any glory with our depleting funds and all this wasted time?*

We learned more about our faith, our love for each other, and how much God really loved us during this time. It wasn't pretty, but God was doing a work in our lives. Six months took us to summertime, and the employment outlook slowed from a crawl to a halt. The unemployment checks stopped, and the severance pay dwindled away. Amazingly enough, the companies that had openings were thinking about their vacations and spending time with their families, not giving one thought to Jim and his need to have a job. *How thoughtless of them*, was my response. We really had to work at not losing sight of the victory. Our emotions were on a roller coaster. What little money we had left was to feed and clothe us and keep a roof over our heads, so there was no thought whatsoever of vacation time. Fortunately, we were very blessed to have family living nearby and spent time with them, but the empty hole of unemployment was always there. Not knowing where or when a job opportunity would come our way or if we would have to move made it very hard to remain cheerful and even pleasant at times. It was like this pain in your head that never went away no matter how many pain relievers you took. Certainly, we trusted God. Certainly, we loved him, and we were pretty sure he loved us. I mentioned *pretty sure* because your mind goes to, *If God loves us so much, how come he doesn't get us out of this?* Or my personal favorite, *Have I been so bad that God would move me to Timbuktu?* When Jim and I would take our evening walks, I would often say that very phrase: "Have I been so bad that God would have to move us so far away from my kids, grandkids, and the area we love?" Then one night, I actually heard what I was saying. It was really such a bizarre statement that when I finally heard myself, I truly thought something was seriously wrong with me. By this time, Jim had interviewed in several states, and there was a strong possibility we would have to move away. But for some reason, I thought we would have to move because I had done something wrong, totally forgetting the fact that it was my husband's unemployment that got us in this situation. *My, this will take some prayer and serious contemplation*, I thought.

A year before this journey started, I had encountered a ministry tool that dealt with healing past memories. I learned that the child you were is the adult you become. We tend to filter many of our adult thoughts through our childhood experiences, good and bad.

Have you ever said, "That person is acting just like a child"? Well, they may have never grown beyond a particular incident in their childhood due to something that affected them. This bizarre line of thinking that it was my fault and I was being punished led me to understand I was reliving my current situation through a childhood experience. My thoughts were not rational, and I was having an extremely emotional response to the thought of moving. Sure, nobody likes change and especially moving; but my response to it was that I must have been so bad that I should be punished, and my punishment was banishment.

During that time, my sister was visiting me from Tampa. She is a pastor and has dealt with others regarding the healing of past memories. She identified that I needed to pray and ask the Holy Spirit to show me what memories were attached to these emotions. I should tell you that when you want to get down to business with God, he more than wants to saddle up next to you and help you through it. The Holy Spirit started revealing certain memories, and I could literally hear some of the words spoken over my young life. Words that caused me to believe the way the enemy wanted. As a young child, I literally felt it was all my fault that we moved so many times and not the truth, which was due to my dad's jobs. Now that's stinking thinking!

Hindsight Diary 10

Not Forsaking the Assembling of Ourselves

There is wisdom in a multitude of counselors. Think of it this way: life is like a bunch of bananas; the one that gets eaten is the one picked from the bunch. We are not meant to go through it alone. Wisdom says to stay in the bunch. Assemble with other believers, do not go through it alone. Write about times you went out on your own and how it would have been better if you had stayed with the bunch.

What the Enemy Means for Bad, God Means for Good

We have an enemy, and he wants to kill, steal, and destroy us. His whole identity is wrapped up in lies. In fact, he is called the "father of lies," and he waits for opportunities to turn innocent statements and thoughts into falsehoods that will totally change the course of your life. A simple statement like, "This will be good for you," or "You can have a fresh start and make new friends," was twisted by the devil to make me feel like I had done something so wrong that my parents must move away and start all over again, like in a witness protection program. These were the lies the enemy whispered to my young, trusting heart when I was growing up. I was five, seven, and nine years old; what kind of fresh start does a young child need? I now know it was the only way my folks felt that they could handle our constant moves, but I only understood it in the way the devil whispered his twisted lies to me. I thought all this moving from state to state was my fault.

The very thought of the possibility of moving in my adult life after we had worked so hard at being planted and involved made me think it must be my fault again. I opened myself up to the fear of separation from my family and the life I love, and the enemy was drooling at the thought of fresh meat served up on a platter of fear. The thoughts of leaving home drove me to my knees but God met me there. He told me it wasn't my fault and he was in control. He had a plan and purpose in all of these moves. My parents' words began to fade away with the reality they did not mean it the way the enemy whispered it to me, and the Lord showed me why my parents chose to look at life through fresh starts. Forgiveness flooded my soul, and I felt such great compassion for my mom and dad. The truth of the situation truly set me free.

I learned we have to be so careful how and who we listen to. It is important to guard our thoughts and sift them through the filters of God's word and not through our childhood memories. I can thankfully say when the lies from the enemy are exposed and brought out into the light, it is a freeing experience. Understanding what the word of God says helps us to hear and recognize his voice more clearly.

Hindsight Diary 11

What the Enemy Means for Bad, God Means for Good

"We are assured and know that [God being a partner in their labor] all things work together and are [fitting into a plan] for good to and for those who love God and are called according to [His] design and purpose" (Rom. 8:28, TAB). Satan knows you are saved and your eternity is sealed, but he will do his very best to make you ineffective. I call Romans 8:28 God's plan B. He will take the bad and turn it to the good if you let him. God always knows the best way for us, so relax and trust him. Don't let the enemy get you sidetracked; stay on track with God and his word. Can you remember a time when you thought you were doing the right thing and it turned out to be the exact opposite? Looking back in hindsight, can you see where you got off the path? God will show you steps to get back on the right path; write down what those steps would be.

Many Are the Plans a Man Has in His Heart

During this time, we had the privilege to listen to many great preachers. Our church, due to its size, was able to bring in some well-known speakers that have a great understanding of the word of God. It was during this time that we heard a teaching on God's promises becoming our own prophecy. God's word is a promise to all who believe. But on occasion, a scripture will just jump out at you while reading the Bible, as if it was written just for you. This particular teaching series was on the favor of the Lord and how he has stored up an abundance of favors for us that will cause us to prosper and add no sorrow to it. Proverbs 10:22 literally leapt off the pages of the Bible for Jim and me. We believed wherever God chose to plant us, we would have *no* sorrow. We could trust him in this and our future. The Lord really did love us, and he would not put Jim and me any place where there would be sorrow added to it. That was God's word, and it is always true. That does not mean it was a smooth ride from there on. But in my heart, I knew everything was going to be all right. Isn't it amazing what you will do when you have to? This was becoming what the Bible refers to as our altar experience. Laying it all down and picking up the cross. We wanted to do this God's way, so we decided to just trust in his word. We collected unemployment for the allotted twenty-six weeks, and my salary at the church kept us going. However, when we reached the ninth month, it started getting tight. My trips to the grocery store usually brought tears on the way home. I would wander up and down the aisle, trying to plan my menus on the sale items. I had always been frugal, but now I had to be exceptionally careful with our finances. By the time I was done at the store, I would climb into the car and cry. I was exhausted and full of care. I would come home and unload the groceries, making sure Jim did not see my red eyes from the drive home. Then I would get to the bedroom to change out of my work clothes and catch a glimpse of the floor next to my bed. It would call out to me, *I need to hear your voice, Father.* As I knelt on the floor, the Lord would hold me in his arms and whisper, "Hold on, Cindy. Hold on to my promises." Then he would tell me to stand up and look out the window. I would hear his familiar phrase, "What do you see?"

The view out the window was of the acreage behind our home. It had been excavated long ago for a development but had turned into small rolling hills of stub grasses where the birds and coyotes loved to roam. When I heard his question again of what do I see, I again said, "Nothing." Then I heard the Lord speaking gently to my heart. "Just because you don't see anything does not mean there is not a master plan." A master plan, yes, there is always a master plan, designed by the Master of all creation. Just because we do not see it does not mean it isn't there. Then he spoke to me again and said, "By the end of summer, you will see activity on this property, and things will begin to move forward for Jim."

Hope came alive in me. I heard his still small voice in the storm, and it quieted my soul. I could still hear the faint sound of the young lions roaring with their lies of destruction and fear, but God's voice was clear and sweet and present. I was learning to trust what I heard in the quietness of my soul. So I watched that acreage behind our property like never before. I shared with Jim, my family, and my closest of friends what I believed the Lord had said. Some of them thought I was nuts, but they agreed God surely must have a master plan, and it would be for our good.

That was a very long summer. There was no activity in the job market at all for my experienced papermaking husband. Every day, I would go off to work in the ministry center; and every day, Jim would go in to his office at home and look for a job. I was very excited when the end of August and Labor Day weekend arrived. This was the end of summer in Michigan. The kids went back to school, things settled down, and I held God's promise close to my heart. I pondered what God had told me—by the end of summer, we will see activity on the land, and it will coincide with activity for Jim's job prospects. I watched that property behind our house like a hawk. I don't know what I was expecting to see, but I knew something was going to happen. In fact, I probably spent far too much time in front of the window gazing at the empty land, waiting to see something—anything. Then

Labor Day came and left and nothing happened. Did I not hear God's voice? I went to my bedroom window fearful I had not heard him correctly. Then I heard his voice again: "It isn't the end of summer yet."

Isn't it amazing how small our minds are? We only believe what we can see or what we think we know to be true. We hear through the filters of what we perceive to be reality and from our personal experiences. For us here in Michigan, summer is over after Labor Day weekend, but the calendar says it's not until September 21. I had a few more weeks to go.

Hindsight Diary 12

Many Are the Plans a Man Has in His Heart

God's ways are far above our ways. He knows our beginning from the end. Remember, he created you. We are to make plans for sure, but it is the Lord who will direct your steps. You cannot turn a bicycle unless you pedal. You just need to keep pedaling and doing the right thing, and the Lord will guide you. Sometimes, it's not doing the wrong thing but just not doing the right thing long enough. Is there something God has asked you to do but you want to give up? Write about it now in your journal. And don't give up!

Hearing God's Voice

How many times do we think we are ready and then we realize we are not? I'm guilty as charged. I'll tell Jim I'm ready to go, he will get in the car, and then I make him wait another five minutes until I climb in. I thought I was ready, but there's always one more thing to do, one more light to turn off. I thought I was ready, but not quite.

I was in my home office preparing to leave for work when I heard Jim call for me to come and look out the back window. Not thinking anything unusual about his request, I peered out over the vast wasteland behind our home. At first I didn't see anything other than the usual bird or wildlife scampering about; then on closer inspection, way off in the distance at the back of the of property, I saw dust rising up from the ground and swirling around. As I peered with more intensity. I could see huge earthmovers the size of dinosaurs roaming over that barren piece of property, the same piece of property God told me to watch! This was the activity God had promised me. I ran to the calendar—it was September 21, the official last day of summer. Jim and I stood there in awe, watching those monstrous mechanical dinosaurs making a way to build a new road. Then I heard his voice again, "When the road is done, it will be over." It was indeed the *last* day of summer. To hear the Lord's voice is more important to me than anything. I had a friend say to me once, "It really scares me that you can hear God's voice." I replied, "It would really scare me if I didn't hear his voice." I know that some will say that I am a little weird. However, if you believe the Bible is the word of God, and the word of God says, "My sheep hear My voice" (John 10:27, NKJV), and we have all been described as his sheep, then we should *all* be hearing his voice, right? Many will say they feel God's presence in nature and through others—and I agree we all can sense his presence that way—but God's Word says we can hear his *voice*. Hearing the voice of God is like hearing your own parents' voice. If they call you on the phone, you don't need to ask them who's calling. You know their voice because you have a relationship with them. You recognize the tone of their voice and their voice patterns. This is also key in learning how to discern the voice of God. You must be in a relationship with him through reading his word in the Bible. You will find that his voice sounds just like his word! For example, in reading this book, you will find I write just like I talk. If you were to meet me in person after reading this, you would recognize my voice through the pages of this book.

That day, the earthmovers began clearing the field for the infrastructure to be laid behind our house, simultaneously the activity in the paper industry began to pick up, just like God promised me. More jobs were posted on the industry's Web sites, and Jim was actually getting responses from his resumes. Unfortunately, most of the jobs were not in Michigan though; but it was activity, and we were prepared to do what we had to do. There was some local activity but very far-fetched and with companies that were not doing very well and struggling to survive. It was hard to get excited about joining a company that was already sinking, but still it was something, and we were leaving no stone unturned. We watched the city facilities come through as they prepared the road behind our house, knowing their activity was parallel to what God was doing for Jim in the job market. The construction crew worked on the infrastructure, just like God was working on ours. The calls started coming in, and Jim began traveling to the southern states and out west, interviewing for the few jobs that were available. Companies were beginning to hire again, so we knew it would just be a matter of time. After all, how long does it take to build a road anyway? Fall was nearly over by now, and we could feel the cold wind of winter coming. I was concerned that the men working on the road wouldn't have enough warm weather left to lay asphalt. After all, one year of unemployment was enough. *We surely have learned all the lessons that we need to, the funds were running out, and, okay, God, please do not forget about us. I know you're really busy and all, but Christmas is coming, and it would really stink if we were unemployed for our second holiday season.*

We found it is very rare for companies to interview let alone hire near the holidays. They are wrapping up their fourth quarters and preparing for the new year, and after all, they have their families, holiday plans, and vacation time to use up before the end of the year. So you guessed it—we went through another holiday without a job for

Jim. This was a tough time for both of us. I received a small bonus for Christmas, so we were able to buy some gifts for our children and grandchildren. I was able to take advantage of sales and bargains, but there was no gift-giving for Jim and me again.

Oh, I know we can get all self-righteous and say it's not the gift but the thought that counts, spending time together as a family—which is true. But come on now, let's be honest—it is about the gifts too, and frankly, it was tough.

All through this time of downsizing, we made every effort to not miss giving our tithe and offerings for the new building at church. We firmly believed that if we helped build God's house, he would continue to build ours. So Jim and I would delay our Christmas gifts again this year. It was okay—tough, but okay. Meanwhile, the construction crews were still slowly working on the land behind our home, and thankfully, there was some activity in the job market. It will just be a matter of time now.

Hindsight Diary 13

Hearing God's Voice

How to recognize God's voice. There is a scripture in the Bible that talks about the wind, in that you can't see it, but you can see the effect of it. This might help you in understanding the voice of God. The Bible says everyone can hear his voice, so it will be a sound that you will recognize. He's very personal. The way you know it is his voice is the effect it will have on you. When the wind blows, it stirs things up like dust and leaves etc. In many ways, God's voice is like the wind—it will move you in your heart as well as stir a peaceful feeling down in your soul. You may even notice a smile cross your face. That's him speaking to you. The Bible says, "Be still and know that I am God" (Ps. 46:10, NKJV). Now take time to be still and listen then write down the first thing you hear. Did it move you? Do you feel his peace? Be still and know.

Laying Down Preconceived Notions

This was a time when we had to throw out all preconceived thoughts and trust the Lord like never before. The money was almost gone, and we were going to have to sell our home within months if something did not happen. Then Jim did our taxes. Because we had been faithful to continue with our tithe and offerings, our tax refund was enough to hold us through another three months. This only delayed the decision to sell the house, but it gave us some breathing room. We tightened our belts even more and pressed into the word of God closer than ever. This was a fight to the finish, and we could almost see the finish line. But then came the flurry of a Michigan winter, and the finish line was covered with fine white crystals of icy snow. All production stopped on the property behind us, and we would not see the dirt again for several months. Thank God, activity continued in Jim's pursuit of gainful employment though. It was slow, but there was activity. Just before the holidays, Jim interviewed in Idaho. It was beautiful territory and a good job. Jim spent three days out there with interviews and toured the area with a realtor. He brought back brochures, and the scenery was breathtaking. But it was so far away, a thirty-three hour drive or half a day by air. Several days later, we got the call from the recruiter. Jim was one out of three, but it was the answer of employment for someone else, not for Jim. We were disappointed and relieved at the same time; Idaho was so far away from home.

Through this time, we could feel momentum picking up. Just before the holidays, we had heard of another potential position in Maine, which was a whole lot closer than Idaho. We went through our holiday knowing our next Christmas might be spent traveling back to Michigan from someplace far away. The New Year brought an interview for the Maine position. There was a paper mill based at the foot of the Appalachian Mountains in need of a product development manager. The interviews went very well. This opportunity looked like it may be more than just an opportunity but a real offer of employment. Would we take it? We had few options. We could sell our house, maybe rent an apartment; then the unfortunate realization hit that I did not make enough to pay the rent on an apartment or even qualify for rental property. Remember, working for the church is usually ministry, not much money. However, we continued to trust what the word of God said, "The steps of a good man are ordered by the lord" (Ps. 37:23). so we decided to take this step of faith, trusting that God would show us what the next step would be, whether it be Maine or Timbuktu.

Jim had several interviews for the position in Maine. He actually had to travel to their corporate office in

Wisconsin a couple of times as well. It seemed like they were really taking their time, and our time was running out.

I was just finishing up a ministry call at work when Jim walked into my office a few weeks after his last interview for Maine. He had a sport coat on and really looked great, but his eyes were red. I jumped out of my chair and ran to him. I was so worried; he looked like he had been crying, and this was a man who did not cry. My heart and mind were racing. We went out into the hallway for some privacy and he said, "I guess we are moving to Maine." I was stunned. My husband finally had a job. Somebody wanted us. After all this time, we were employed, but Maine? We cried together in the hallway, out of relief and joy that our season was finally over. We would start a new life together in the pristine wilderness of New England. It would be okay. God promised that he would cause us to prosper and add no sorrow to it. Then Jim presented me with a lovely gift. He had gone to the jewelry store and bought me a watch because mine had died and we were not able to afford a new one. Bless his heart—he just wanted to finally buy me something. The watch was symbolic of all the time that had gone by and much more to come. Jim and I walked back into the office to share our great news, news of his new employment, but also the news we would be moving to Maine. My boss, Deb, and coworker Cindy were in the office, having a mini meeting with our IT department. I could not wait to share, so we barged into their meeting. There were cries of joy and of sadness too. These were my best friends, and we knew this meant much more than a job, but it would be a change of life. We felt joy for the victory of employment after sixteen long months, but now we had to face the facts. I would be leaving. We had talked about the possibility of us moving, but my boss never wanted to pursue the subject of my replacement until we knew for sure. Well, we knew for sure now, and it was time to start preparing for my departure.

This was a big step for us. The company that hired Jim would help with our relocation, the selling of our current home, and a house-hunting trip. However, they wanted Jim to start as soon as possible. They had taken their own sweet time during the interview process, and now they wanted us to find a home and temporary housing to start work in three weeks. We had to move quickly. Flight arrangements were made to go to Maine for house hunting. When Jim interviewed before, he went alone and said the countryside was beautiful; and of course, everything we heard and saw in books about Maine was wonderful. Our youngest son even bought us a book all about Maine, and I surfed the Internet and researched the area, housing, and churches. It was a long way away from family, but we believed God's promises are true, and I was going to hold him to his word. Within seven days, we would be flying off to find our new home out east. We booked flights quickly and had to take first-class seats on the way home due to availability. The company would pay for the trip, so when you have to move fast, you have to take what is available. Little did we know, those first-class tickets on our return trip would be a godsend.

My mom and stepdad were passing through that day on their snowbird return from the South, so we went out to dinner with them to celebrate. While we were out dining, talking, and making plans for this brave new world in Maine, Jim's father left an interesting message on our answering machine. His dad decided to surf the Internet job sites one more time, hoping to find a papermaking position in Michigan for his firstborn. He knew that we were up for the challenge in Maine but thought he would look just one more time. I'll never forget the message he left on our answering machine. "Hey, Jim, this is your dad. I don't want to muck things up for you, but I found a position in West Michigan that looked like they used your resume to write the job description and maybe you should take a look at it?" *What? A job in Michigan, a stone left unturned?*

Our first response was, "Oh no, this might be a distraction." Even our well-meaning friends thought the same thing. But Jim said he would check it out just in case. It seemed very far-fetched because he knew every paper mill in West Michigan, and it did not sound like any mill he knew about. It was most likely a fishing expedition from some recruiter trying to get leads. He called and left a message regarding his interest with the recruiter's voicemail on Friday. Saturday morning, the phone rang. It was the recruiter. As Jim spoke with him, I felt a strange stirring inside—a feeling I had not felt in a long time. It was like this bubbling up of hope, a hope that West Michigan had not abandoned us but maybe was just overlooked or hidden—like when you are looking for something important, and, in your haste, you just miss it; but on second glance, there it was. And there it was, indeed. The position was real, and Jim's resume did fit the qualifications as if the position was tailor-made just for him.

We were scheduled to fly off to the East Coast for Maine on Monday, and Jim and I had to be on that plane. We made a commitment, the tickets had been purchased, and we had to walk this out. A bird in the hand is still better than one in the bush they say, but my heart and head were in two different states. My head said we were flying to Maine to find our new home; we have a job there. But my heart was saying, "God, please don't move us away from Michigan and everything that is precious to us." All along, there was this little seed of hope growing in our hearts. We laid everything on the altar: our lives, our children and grandchildren, our families, our home, and our church. We were very open to the fact that God could be in Maine for us, but our hearts were ever hopeful toward our Mitten State.

It was an easy flight into Portland. We saw the beautiful countryside and, of course, the breathtaking coastline from the plane's windows. We picked up our rental car and started the one-and-a-half-hour drive back into the interior of Maine, the foothills of the Appalachian Mountains where our new home might be. We arrived midafternoon in central Maine with enough time to drive around and get a general feel of the area. This was mid-April, and winter was just exiting; so it was cold, damp, and a bit gray. The landscape was beautiful in some places but quite depressing in others. The housing market seemed to be very limited; they had not undergone the housing boom that West Michigan was experiencing, and finding what we wanted in a home might be a challenge. We met with our designated realtor that afternoon, and he gave us maps and an itinerary for the next couple of days of house hunting.

We drove back to our hotel to unpack and discuss our day's events. Jim is a quiet man, but he was unusually quiet that day. I did not have much to say either. Central Maine was not what we expected. We were hungry and tired from our trip, so we decided to dine in at the hotel's restaurant. The hotel was old and in great need of a face-lift, but the room was warm after the manager jump-started the heater. The décor was from the sixties and seventies as well as the music playing at the restaurant. We felt like we had gone through some kind of a backward time warp, but these two starving Midwesterners just wanted some good food. We were in Maine, so there should be great seafood on the menu, right? We took a look at the buffet to see if we should order off the menu or take the steam table. The buffet supplied the regular fare of beef tips, mashed potatoes, fish, and fried chicken. But we were on the East Coast, so it was good eats off the menu for us tonight. The waitress stopped by with our water, and we said we would pass on the buffet tonight and would like a menu please. "Menu? We only have the buffet," said the cute little waitress with a look on her face that said, *You're not from around hearaa.* We found that phrase would dominate a great deal of our trip while in central Maine. I should mention, before I continue on in our experience in the great Northeast, that I'm sure there are wonderful people in Maine; unfortunately we just didn't encounter many. "Only the buffet," I said. "What about lobster?"

"Oh, it's out of season," she replied with the face that said, *Tourists.* I looked at Jim across the table, and he had a look on his face that I did not know if he was going to laugh or cry. I said to him, fighting back my own emotions, "What weeere you thinking?" His eyes were as big as silver dollars and glazing over with tears. He was holding back laughter, and I thought he was going to explode because this situation all seemed so unbelievable. The hotel was run-down and it was one of the better ones in the area, and *no* seafood on top of everything else? We were in the land of buffets and steam tables. The housing was subpar, and the countryside was littered with garbage and debris, which they called "pride of ownership"? Heaven help us, we were in a foreign land and definitely "not from around hearaa." Jim said he had been silent because he wanted to know my reaction before he said anything. My reaction was just laughter; when it gets that bad, tears will not do, unless they are tears of joy. I knew God was up to something, and this was hilarious.

Hindsight Diary 14.

Laying Down Preconceived Notions

The Lord works in mysterious ways, and his thoughts are far above our thoughts. We miss it because we usually think much smaller than God. He has great plans for us, and we settle for small leftovers. The Lord has called us to his banquet table. Often, we settle for just a chicken wing when he wants us to have the whole bird. Laying down preconceived notions about yourself and your abilities is hard. But remember this: the Lord is not looking at your ability but your availability. Have you ever settled for something less knowing there was something better just around the corner? Write about it and discover ways God can redeem it.

Your Response Determines Your Results

"The blessing of the lord makes one rich, and He adds no sorrow with it" (Prov. 10:22, NKJV). This was a promise from God that I stood on and believed, so much so that I think God wrote it just for me. It was money in the bank and I was cashing in. "God, you are faithful, and you said we will prosper and have no sorrow; so if Maine is where Jim and I will be hanging our hat, then, by God, we will be happy."

And happy we were; everything was funny to us. Don't get me wrong, it was not pleasant, but God had turned our perspective around. We knew the Lord would not let us down, and he would show us what we needed to see. Jim's silence was broken. He confessed that he was so focused on the job opportunity and the fact he hadn't had a job for sixteen months that he really did not see what the area was truly like. I totally understood, and we agreed to trust the Lord and really pray that the door would be open for us to stay in West Michigan. "But not our will be done, but yours, oh Lord."

Our reaction to this part of our journey was what God was watching for. "Will you lay it all down? Will you move here? Will you leave your family and friends, church, your lives, and follow me here to the utter ends of the earth?"

"Yes, Lord, if this is what you want us to do, we choose to trust you, knowing fully there will be no sorrow here in the land of 'pride of ownership.'" This was really where the rubber-meets-the-road kind of faith. But when you choose to obey, the Lord comes in with a peace that you cannot explain, and the joy of the Lord becomes your strength.

The steam table fare was filling, and not all that bad. Jim and I were enjoying each other's company and looked forward to another day of adventure. My heart was still in West Michigan, and my eyes continually looked at Maine through that filter, but I tried to remain open and willing to see if God was there in Maine for us. We started out with a trip to visit the realtor that had been assigned to us. He took us down to the basement of his office—which was cold and barren—and showed us pictures of the homes we were to preview. *This was going to be different*. We had made a list of specifics we were looking for in a home, and apparently, he didn't get the memo because each listing was really different from what we said we would consider. He assured us that we would like these homes, and he had already made arrangements with the homeowners to preview their residences. And, after all, it would give us a good feel for the area. So we all got in the realtor's car to start our adventure, with Jim in the front seat and me in the back so I could get a good view and pray. This was the realtor's winter car, and it was running on a hope and a prayer. I don't think he had cleaned it since he bought it several years ago, and why bother cleaning the windshield when it's just going to get dirty again anyway? I just chuckled in the backseat. Jim could hear me, and he knew I was okay as long as I kept laughing. He had to really work at maintaining his joy as well, and we continued to focus on the opportunity set before us. It was the bird in the hand right now, and we must press on with what we had while looking in the bush.

The houses were all old, in need of repair, and costly. We thought we had made it clear to the realtor that we did not want a fixer-upper at this stage of our lives, and we preferred to stay on a tighter budget. We explained that we had just built a house and wanted something of that quality. Apparently the housing market in central Maine was not like the one in West Michigan, but they did have some vacant lots. So the next day, the realtor helped us look at a few more houses and land for sale. You could tell the realtor was getting upset with us on our likes and dislikes, but what are you going to do? We had this "no sorrow" attitude, and from our vantage point, there was much sorrow looking at these homes that needed repair and were in places we did not want to locate, like next door to a "pride of ownership" house that showed no pride whatsoever. The last house we looked at had a great view, overlooking some wonderful hills and valleys, but the home itself just did not fit the type of life we wanted. That is when the realtor made a fatal error. While I was looking out the window admiring the view and trying to explain in the kindest of terms that this was not the type of home we wanted, another fixer-upper, he said, "Well, you are going to have to settle because you're homeless." Jim turned quickly to hopefully deflect the wrath that was coming this man's way as I turned in the realtor's direction, saying in my low mother-type voice that still sends the hair up on the back of my kids' necks, "I'm not homeless Yet!" The realtor immediately knew in no uncertain terms what I meant. *I am not homeless, and I never will be, and you just lost your sale buddy!* We were so done looking at homes. We came to the conclusion that if God wanted us to live here, we would have to build again. So the next day, we spent looking at some land. The realtor showed us where there were some developments popping up and gave us some listings of other locations but shared with us where we would and would not want to build because this area was home to one of the world's largest manufacturer of brown eggs. You see, there is an industry in that area that stinks more than paper mills, and it is chickens. I don't know if you have ever experienced the aroma of a chicken farm, but if you have, it is unforgettable. You know you are getting close just by the pungent smell within ten miles of the facility. And unfortunately, the property that was available in the area where we were to locate was within that ten-mile radius. Jim and I drove to these lovely lots and gazed out our rental car's clean windshield at the fantastic views of the snowcapped mountains and got out of the car to enjoy the view, thinking we could handle living there. Then within a few steps away from the vehicle, we looked at each other and said, "What is that smell?" There was this prevalent odor that permeated the entire area, even without a prevailing wind. You could not get away from it. No wonder the lots were so reasonably priced, with great views and the smell of chicken poop. Trust me, this is not a smell that you can ever get used to; and to make matters worse, the realtor said that this particular chicken farmer was a real entrepreneur too; he sells the chicken manure as fertilizer to the surrounding farmers so they can spread it on their fields in the spring. Oh yeah, what a deal!

Just as we were pulling out of the last development with the beautiful stinking lots, Jim's cell phone rang. At that moment, it was the sweetest noise I'd ever heard. It was the recruiter telling Jim he lined up an interview for the West Michigan location on the Monday after we returned from Maine. There was an explosion of hope in that rental car that lit up the atmosphere. My heart literally leapt, and Jim and I were filled with thankfulness for an open door in just the nick of time. We wondered, could this be our ram in the thicket like Abraham's test in the Bible? God told Abraham to offer up Isaac as a sacrifice, and at the very last moment, the Lord provided a ram instead. Maybe this was what the Lord was asking of Jim and me. Were we willing to lay Michigan on the altar and trust him?

Hindsight Diary 15

Your Response Determines Your Results

What does faith say? This must be your response in all situations. We are born on this earth with a natural tendency to be negative. That natural tendency is totally contrary to God. He is always positive. We must control our tongue as it sets the course of our life, just like the rudder of a ship. To determine your direction, you must speak what God speaks. What direction do you want to go? Do you have a situation in your life right now that is not going in the direction you want it to go? Find a promise from God and write down both the situation and the promise. Let's see what God has to say about the matter.

The Altar Experience

That one phone call led to more during the rest of the week. Jim talked to their HR person to set up interview arrangements in Michigan upon our return. We had a time-sensitive issue with Maine, and if this was going to work, the interviews would have to move quickly. While we were in Maine, Jim was to have the company on-site physical, so we had to continue with what we had in our hand. But there was hope blooming in our hearts again for West Michigan. All went well with the physical, and we met with the Maine HR director. He was a very nice man. This facility was your typical old paper mill sitting next to a roaring river. Not a glamorous job, but a job that Jim always did well and enjoyed. The little town where the paper mill was located had a very New England feel to it. Life would certainly be different here for us. However, in our hearts we now had hope, like a flower blossoming in early spring. The lenses from which we viewed everything seemed to have changed. We were once again looking with hope to Michigan; after all, "faith is the substance of things hoped for, the evidence of things not seen" (Heb. 11:1, NKJV). Hope was blooming again in our hearts.

The calls from the recruiter and the HR manager for the Michigan opportunity were frequent and very encouraging. They were all amazed at how perfectly Jim fit their job description. All his experience and background were exactly what they were looking for. Our hearts were filled with wonder and awe of the timing.

Sometimes God has to take you to the altar. Are we really willing to give it all to him? We can get this mindset that God is trying to take something from us and is up there in heaven, waiting for something good to happen to us, just so he can take it away. Or maybe, God is really not all that interested in our little lives down here. There are even times when we question if there really is a God, and if there is, why isn't he doing something about this fix we're in? *I thought you loved us, God?* At some point, we all have one or more of those thoughts. That is where the battle is. We let our thoughts and feelings get the better of us. It is only through studying the word of God that we can gain control those thoughts. It is important to replace those thoughts and feelings of doubt and unbelief by accepting what He wrote in his love letters to us in the Bible. He is for us and not against us. We need to get it into our heads and down to our hearts. God Almighty loves us and only wants the very best for us. We have to get over the feelings and thoughts that are against us and press into the words that God says about us: "Because he has set his love upon Me, therefore will I deliver him; I will set him on high, because he knows and understands My name [has a personal knowledge of My mercy, love, and kindness—trusts and relies on Me, knowing I will never forsake him, no, never]" (Ps. 91:14, TAB). That scripture puts it so wonderfully—"because he knows and understands My name." We can know God because of what his word says about him, and he will deliver us and set our feet in a secure place.

The week in Maine was an adventure in comedy, futility, and patience. We could not find housing, bathrooms, or cordial people. After three days of looking for a house, we decided to head back toward Portland to enjoy the scenery and food, get some rest, and go home, trusting that the Lord was opening a door back to our homeland.

Hindsight Diary 16

The Altar Experience

In order to follow the Lord, we must all, at one time or another, come to the altar. The letting-go process is difficult, and many times you may think you have laid it down just to pick it up again. The Lord has many promises in his word that says if you lay it down, he will give it back to you. God is not interested in your stuff; he just doesn't want your stuff to have you. He is a jealous God and wants nothing to come between you and him. If your stuff is more important than spending time with him, then your stuff has taken his place. It is a matter of priorities. Keep them straight and you can keep your stuff. Just be sure to have a For Sale sign handy. What are you most attached to? Could you let it go if it was asked of you?

Things Are Not What They Appear

We finally found a nice restaurant in Portland on our last night in Maine and had our elusive lobster dinner. We could leave now, full and complete, knowing we had done our best to try to find housing and to make this thing work. We packed our bags and went to bed, thankful that we were going back home. We had to get up very early the next morning for our flight out, but I was up well before the alarm went off. My stomach was in knots. I first thought it was nerves, but within minutes, I knew I was in trouble.

After several trips to the bathroom in the dark, I had lost the illusive lobster I had waited all week to consume. In fact, I lost the lunch and breakfast from the previous day and, quite possibly my toenails too. Thankful that I was getting it all out of my system before we left, I went back to bed for a quick snooze before the alarm went off. Upon rising again, I found myself running back into the bathroom for another round of the old heave-ho. Nothing was going to keep me from going home, not even food poisoning. We had more than an hour's wait in the

Portland airport before we could board the plane. My time was spent in the public restroom, putting my face where no face should go in public or any bathroom for that matter. Thankfully, we were boarded in first class on the return trip. Of course, by now the food poisoning had reached my lower intestines, so I was having two cleansings for the price of one first-class ticket. Again, I was just so thankful to be heading home and the added blessing of being seated only one step away from the airplane lavatory. I spent most of the flight in there. The little restroom was so accommodating. You could barf and sit at the same time. Disgusting, I know, but I was just thankful for the convenience as well as the loudness of the airplane so the other passengers could not hear the unbelievable noises that I didn't even know I could make. It was bad! Poor Jim. I'm sure he was embarrassed for himself and for me, but there was absolutely nothing I could do. It seemed as though I was purging Maine from my system. By the time we got to Detroit, there was not much left in me. I was so weak that Jim had to almost carry me to the next gate in the terminal. Thank God we did not have to walk far. I put in a call to my sister from my cell phone for prayer. I was so sick and weak but still very thankful to be back on Michigan soil. The trip to Grand Rapids from Detroit is a quick one, which was good because there was no assessable bathroom on the small plane. I managed to hold it together for the forty-five-minute flight. Jim helped me off the plane, and I almost lost it while walking down the gate to retrieve our bags. All I could say was, "I'm never leaving West Michigan again." I wanted to kiss the ground. I don't think I've ever been so sick in my life. There was no trace of Maine left in my body, and I thanked Jesus for bringing me back home alive.

The interesting thing about food poisoning is that when you finally get it all out of your system, you are fine. You feel like you have gone through a boxing match with the devil, but you are alive and can begin functioning again; this was good because Jim and I had some plans the next day that would trim our sails again in this adventure, and they did not include lobster!

While we were in Maine, Jim was in constant communication with the recruiter for the opportunity in Michigan. He landed a meeting quickly, and they were preparing for his interview process. The company was willing to move fast if they liked what they saw. We flew home from Maine on Saturday; then Sunday after church, Jim and I drove south to the town where the position was located. The mapping program said it was an hour and a half drive, but we thought it was closer; so to make sure, we decided to drive down to Michigan's great southwest.

Hindsight Diary 17

Things Are Not What They Appear

The Lord promises in Jeremiah 33:3 that if you call upon him, he will reveal hidden things to you. This is very important because so many things are not what they appear. The Lord will also reveal your own motives if you ask him. If something does not feel right, ask. He has put those feelings inside of you to give you a warning. Pay attention to that still small voice—it will bring healing and restoration in areas of your life that you did not even know were broken. Write down a few brief times when you felt the Lord's caution on your behavior. Was it a warning?

A Righteous Man's Steps Are Ordered by the Lord

We have learned the first step of favor is being in the right place at the right time. The drive only took one hour. The mapping program said to turn down one particular street, when it should have been another, so we were surprised to end up in a wonderful subdivision of new homes. After we found the facility where Jim's interview would be, we would return and look at these houses. So we turned around and drove into the facility's parking lot. My heart leapt with thankfulness. I don't know if you know what a paper mill looks or smells like, but they are not the most attractive places to work in; although much needed, Jim's profession is far from glamorous. However, this building was not a paper mill. It was a large, lovely, clean building with professional offices and no smell. The facility only coated the paper, it did not make it. Hallelujah! Jim and I got out of the car, placed our feet on the property, and believed God's word that said, "Every place upon which the sole of your foot shall tread, that have I given to you" (Josh. 1:3, TAB). We prayed this was indeed given to us and hopped back in the car and drove around to the area of homes we found *just by accident.* And wouldn't you know it, there was an open house. The house was beautiful and only one street away from the coating facility. We loved the closeness; Jim could walk to work just like he did several years ago when we lived in a small town north of Kalamazoo. The first house we visited was too large for just Jim and me. However, the realtor gave us some interesting information about the area and the homes we just happened to have discovered. This particular location was actually in an enterprise zone, which meant that property taxes were waived for a period of years to encourage population growth. The area had gone through some hard times, and the community was doing what it could to rebuild with incentives to locate locally. As we drove around this small development, we found another open house and decided to take a look. When Jim and I entered, we were taken aback by the home's simplicity and elegance. It was brand new, and the builder was hosting the open house. As we walked through the home, Jim and I were impressed by the layout and design, but it was far more than we thought we could afford. However, it was a beautiful house and very convenient to the facility where Jim was to have his interview the next day. Before leaving the area, we took a drive and felt we had entered into a dream world. Jim and I had always hoped to be close to Lake Michigan but never really thought that would be realistic, so we did not dwell on it. However, here it was, only one hour away from our family and near the lovely community of St. Joseph, one of Michigan's best kept secrets on the shores of Lake Michigan. My heart filled with hope; my cup was overflowing with thankfulness. "Oh God, please let this be your will." His word does say, "Delight yourself also in the lord, and He shall give you the desires of your heart" (Ps. 37:3, NKJV).

I rode home with one purpose in mind: Get Jim ready for the next day and his first interview for this new opportunity. *Lord, you will really have to move fast on this one. Maine thinks Jim will start work in one week.* The realtors had been contacted, and the relocation company for Maine was making arrangements.

Our plan had been for Jim to drive out to Maine and live in temporary housing until our house sold and I would join him. Remember, we had a job in our hand after sixteen months of looking. We had to walk this thing out, trusting that God was in control and taking care of the details, putting one foot in front of the other. Jim was focusing on the new interview, and I was wondering what God was up to.

The recruiter for the position in Michigan was fantastic. He had placed many people with this company and knew the process and the people that Jim would be talking with. He was able to give Jim insight into the business as well as the personality types he would be interviewing. Jim would meet with the plant manager first. If all went well, there would be a few more interviews with upper-level management in a couple of other states where their corporate offices were. I went to work that Monday morning with quite the story to tell my friends.

When I walked into the ministry center, everyone was glad to see me and they had lots of questions about

Maine and our new home. The suspense was so thick you could cut it with a knife. They all said, "So how was Maine?" And I replied very slowly. "It was awful!" They looked at me in shock until I began to tell them the details of our trip out East followed by the phone calls back and forth with the recruiter for the job in Michigan. What we thought might have been a distraction had hopefully turned out to be our ram in the thicket. We believed Maine may have been about laying everything down on the altar for God. We also believed that God was testing us, not for God to find out what was in our hearts, but for us to find out what our hearts desires were. We were willing, but our Heavenly Father is a Good Father, and he already knows what is in our hearts and what is best for us and his kingdom. We were not ready to leave Michigan. The morning went by extremely fast, and before I knew it, Jim was calling from his cell phone, saying his first interview went very well; so well, in fact, that the recruiter called right back and was instructed to set up the second interview in the Carolinas for the next round of corporate-level meetings. "Oh God, you are so faithful," was all I could say. Everyone around me knew we were seeing a miracle taking place right in front of our eyes. After sixteen long months of ups and downs and months of no activity at all, we were in a position of two possible job offers. Now we needed to work on a delay for Jim's start date in Maine. Jim asked for a week's extension. He still had not found housing, which was the truth. We knew we had to tell Maine what was going on. It would not be right to lead them along, and we did not want to lose our blessing from the Lord by being deceptive. We decided when Jim got the dates for the next round of interviews, he would talk with the man he was to report to in Maine. We were still a little gun-shy. We had been told a few times that Jim would have these corporate-level interviews on other occasions, and the process dragged on for months. In fact, that very thing happened with the Maine position. However, I have to tell you—when it is God, it is just right, and usually quick. Two days later, Jim had the interview dates for the next step. We knew we had to let Maine know what was going on now; it was the right thing to do. The man that Jim was to report to in Maine was a very nice person. After hearing our story, he agreed that we should follow through with the interviews for the Michigan position so that we would know for sure which one it was to be. The last person they had in that position did not stay because he and his wife were not able to adapt to the lifestyle of central Maine. He gave us a two-week extension. We would surely know by then. The recruiter did his due diligence and provided Jim with a biography on the gentlemen he would be speaking with. This group of interviewers had nixed the last candidate they spoke with because he did not have enough experience. Jim had worked over thirty years in the paper industry, so that wouldn't be an issue for them this time. We had this undercurrent of knowing God was in control, so Jim wasn't overly nervous. This was a time to lay down our anxieties and focus on the word of God. Jim and I had scriptures that we read daily, and we chose to trust God's word that says, "The steps of a good man are ordered by the lord" (Ps. 37:23, NKJV). We believed God was ordering Jim's steps one by one. Jim was nervous, but confident in God.

We decided to keep the appointment with the realtor to list our current house. They were originally assigned to us with the relocation company for our move to Maine, and we knew that we had to keep moving forward with what we had in our hands. Plus, they had already put work into their marketing ideas, and we might need them anyway if we moved farther down Michigan's shoreline. Also, the movers contacted us and were scheduled to come for a walk-through to see how much stuff we had—which was still far too much. So life was really picking up speed. Everyone at work wanted to know how things were progressing. It was like a huge mystery unfolding before all our eyes. Jim was studying up on the company and its personnel. I was taking inventory of our lives and kept communication open between realtors, movers, and—oh yeah, we were in the process of being approved for a new mortgage out in Maine too. Yes, I was juggling several balls at once. At one point, I had my cell phone headset on one ear and my land phone on the other, talking with two different companies at the same time. Our youngest son was still living with us in the unfinished basement, so he now needed to find another place to live also. That meant, of course, we would have to help him move because they just would not sell our house with a tenant living in the lower level.

Jim's second interview went very well. While flying back home that same afternoon, the recruiter was already calling him during his brief layover in Detroit. Things looked very promising, and it looked like an excellent fit according to the recruiter's comment. They wanted Jim to come back the next week for one more round of interviews in the Carolinas and also in Tennessee, where there was another facility that this position would oversee on a technical basis. The position that Jim was interviewing for was for technical manager over two facilities: the one in Michigan as well as Tennessee. God says he will give you double for your trouble. It was coming to pass, and all I could do for Jim was to keep his clothes cleaned and pressed and prayed up. Over a seventeen-day period, he had eleven corporate-level interviews from Michigan to the Carolinas and Tennessee. Jim was calm and excited at the same time. He was blessed with a supernatural peace that was hard to explain. I was on my face continually in prayer and we had many, many people praying for us. He came home on the sixteenth day after the interview process had started. Maine was still waiting for his response. We were at the end of the interviews for Michigan and waiting for their response. The recruiter for the Michigan position said everything looked like it was a go, and they were even discussing an employment package. It had all the earmarks of an offer.

When I picked Jim up from the airport after his last interview, he tried to relay everything that had happened—all the conversations, questions, and any slight indication of what they were thinking about. Jim knew he had done everything he could; now, it was up to God. We agreed that even though we could sense the low rumble of roaring lions using the devil's lies to try and get a foothold in our thoughts, we would only speak words of faith. If they were not faith-filled words, we would just not speak at all. The devil and doubt felt like bumblebees flying around my head, and I was swatting at them with my little faith-filled fly swatter. The what-ifs were pursuing me with a vengeance, trying to steal my faith and blessing.

Hindsight Diary 18

A Righteous Man's Steps Are Ordered by the Lord

This is an area of trusting God. You do your part, and God will do his. It's important to take steps, sometimes baby steps, trusting that he will direct your path. What what-ifs are you battling? Find your scripture that defines the truth about your "if" and let the scripture battle it.

Though the Vision Tarry

That night, in agony, I chose to stand against all my feelings of fear and doubt and spoke out with a loud voice, "God, I'm hanging on to your promises, and I'm not letting go." Immediately, I had a vision.

I could see Jim and me on a midsized sailboat in open waters. We were in a horrific storm and surrounded in darkness. The rain was pummeling us from all directions with tremendous gusts of wind. We were dressed in full rain gear, head to toe, with Jim at the helm, hanging on to the steering wheel with all his strength, and I was holding on to two ropes in the front of the boat. These ropes were like lifelines with two scriptures written on them: "With favor You will surround him as with a shield" and "The blessing of the lord makes one rich, and He adds no sorrow with it" (Ps. 5:12 and Prov. 10:22, NKJV). While hanging on to those lifelines, I yelled at the top of my lungs just as I had shouted before, "I'm hanging on to your promises, Lord, and I'm not letting go." Instantly, the storm stopped. The darkness became light, and the clouds and the torrents of rain disappeared, showing the brilliant blue sky above. The strong wind that had tossed us about in that massive storm now began to propel us forward at breakneck speed. Our rain gear and hoods were blown off, and we were being driven forward with great force. It was exhilarating; then the vision ended.

I recognized that I had experienced a wonderful revelation from the Lord regarding our situation. I asked him to explain it to me. He told me the storm was over, and he was moving us toward our destiny. However, I had a question about the wind. The same wind that was in the storm was also propelling us forward in good weather. I asked the Lord, *What was the difference between the good weather and bad?* "The pressure," was his reply. It is the barometric pressure that causes weather to be stormy or not. Jim and I were under incredible pressure, and how we would handle it with the confession of our mouth would determine our outcome. The word of God says, "Death and life are in the power of the tongue, and those who love it will eat its fruit" (Prov. 18:21, NKJV). Choosing to follow the Lord and doing it his way will be the hardest and the easiest thing you will ever do. Trusting that he will deliver you, even if you have to sacrifice it all on the altar, is hard. We were willing to lay it all down and move to Maine and leave our treasures behind, trusting the Lord would cause us to prosper and add no sorrow to it. Our storm stopped because of the power of the spoken word of God, and we were being quickly propelled to our promised land. When I think back on that vision, I am in awe of its accuracy. The storm that had raged in the vision was just like the storm we had been living in for seventeen months. Jim was at the helm, steering and charting our way. I was hanging on to the only thing I knew I could trust—the Word of God. I could not trust in man, I could not trust in what I saw, and I certainly could not trust my feelings. Our boat was taking on water, and we were being pitched to and fro with one gust after another. But we continued on together, declaring and trusting in the word of God. What a ride!

I said from the beginning, when Jim was laid off, that I wanted a testimony and I wanted God to get all the glory. I did not want just some ordinary job for Jim, but I wanted him to have the opportunity of a lifetime, believing God would not have us go through such an extraordinary experience to have an ordinary life. I had no idea what was in store for us at that time. God is so awesome. He knows our frame and what we can endure. But we do have to play it by his rules. We must proclaim his promises over our lives. The word of God is his promise for us. God knows our end from our beginning, and we are to live victorious lives. However, to live victoriously means we must also fight the good fight of faith. The Lord said he would fight our battles—and he will. Have you ever watched a battle in a movie? The army stands at the top of the ridge, and the leader declares the victory before they charge. That is what we are to do. Declare the victory, not the problem. That's when the Lord goes before you and fights the battle. You must declare the victory, and your victory cry must be God's promise. Our promise and battle cry was that the Lord would cause us to prosper and add no sorrow.

I knew I would be at work the day the phone call came with the job offer. The recruiter had given us an assurance that it would be Wednesday. Jim had just gotten home on that Tuesday and did not even have time to get his thank-you letters out to those he had spoken with the previous week. I had caller ID on my phone, and when it rang, I knew it was the captain of my ship calling with good news. Jim's voice was so rich with joy and yet so soft and humble. He said they were all very impressed with him and would like to have him start as soon as possible. It was so matter-of-fact. Then he began to tell me of the benefit package and salary, start date, title, and relocation package. The recruiter asked Jim later that day what my response was to his great news. "She was speechless," was his reply, and that's the truth. As Jim relayed the good news, I wrote it down as I always do. Technical manager over two facilities—one in West Michigan, one in Tennessee—full benefits, bonus program, and a great salary, which was seventeen thousand dollars more than the Maine offer and seventeen thousand dollars more than what his previous employer paid him (*this number seventeen must be significant*, I thought), plus a start date with full benefits the first of May and a relocation package that was more than I could have ever dreamed of. I was indeed speechless. God had taken my breath away. We believed God for double for our trouble, and here it was! We couldn't talk long because Jim had many phone calls to make, the first one to Maine. I still had a job to do as best I could without laughing and crying. The storm was gone and the wind picked up speed. I honestly had a hard time talking. To know me is to understand what an oddity that is. I always have something to say. I turned from my desk after hanging up with Jim and went into my boss's office. My coworker and close friend, Cindy, was right behind me. I stood in front of my boss's desk, and as she turned from her computer, she saw the look on my face. I was in shock, in joy, in wonder. I could not talk in complete sentences; I just sputtered out words. All I could say was, "Jim, offer, West Michigan, God is faithful." We had a group hug; we were laughing and crying together. The whole office could hear us by now. These were my best friends, my prayer warriors, and my confidants. Our long journey was over. Yes, there were many things to do now, but the uncertain was now certain. We were out of limbo and back on track, pressing on and staying on West Michigan soil for now.

Jim's call to Maine was very cordial. They really did want the best for us and knew that if it did not work for us there, it would affect them in a negative way in the long run. We, of course, had to pay for the trip out to Maine for house hunting, but we fully believed it was worth the expense (except the food poisoning), and the Lord would provide the funds to take care of it. We were able to retain the same realtors to sell our home that we would have used for moving to Maine, so that saved time and effort.

Jim and I believed that even though his new job was only a one-hour drive from where we were currently living, a commute was not possible with the schedule that he would have to keep. The paper industry demands variable hours, and Jim is not the type of person who enjoys the two-hour drive listening to daily talk radio while commuting back-and-forth to work. Plus, we had already found the house we liked. God had provided Jim's job, salary, and our new home.

The time frame was incredible. Jim got home from the last interview on Tuesday, April 26, received the offer Wednesday, the twenty-seventh, and they wanted him to start Monday, May 2. I looked at the calendar, and it seemed like all these dates had some significance, but I didn't have the time to check it out. I gave my notice at work—three weeks would do, and it should give me enough time to get ready for our move. The relocation company would do most of it for us. I just had to decide what would go and what would not. I had already cleaned and organized my desk at work, but there were still the daily activities and the fine-tuning of my work responsibilities and training my replacement. I put in a full day of work the day Jim got his job offer, but I had to get groceries before coming home. While at the store, my cell phone rang. It was Jim. "Guess what's going on behind our house?" he said. I did not even hesitate. I yelled into the phone loud enough so that just about anyone near me would have heard. "They're paving the road!" No one could have planned that. Only God can orchestrate such a plan. Only God can move those kinds of mountains. Only God alone could time these events to work for his glory and his glory alone. Our role is to give voice to God's word, to believe it and receive it. I remembered what the Lord had told me that day, looking out upon that barren chunk of land, "Just because you do not see anything does not mean there isn't a master plan." The final coat of asphalt was being laid on the road behind our home. God told me when the road was finished, our time of waiting would be done. This was the same day Jim got his job offer. We are moving on; this season really is over. The people at the store must have thought I was nuts, and I was. I was just nuttier than a fruitcake and loving my husband and my God.

I got home as soon as I could. There were tears again in my car after shopping, but this time they were not tears of sadness and despair but joy and thankfulness. *I heard your voice, Father. You have always had us in your loving hands. The times when I saw my husband cry, you were there. The times that I thought I could not take it anymore and I hid in my bedroom sharing with you alone my fears, you were there. During those early morning hours when you would wake me at 3:33 a.m. and I would stumble out of my bed to listen to you, your words would comfort me, saying, "Call to Me, and I will answer you, and show you great and mighty things, which you do not know."*[1] *I would get on my knees and say, like Samuel, "Yes, Lord, your servant is listening," and you would share those great and mighty things with me. You assured me of your love and your sovereignty, and that I must hold on to your promises and declare everything that you have done in my life. You, oh Lord, allowed me to be angry and wrestle with you. You understood my fears and concerns for my husband, my hopes and desires for my children, and my longing to be with and near my grandchildren. You knew I was not ready or able to be apart from my family at this time.*

Jim and I watched as the pavers put the last coat of asphalt on the road behind our house that afternoon. A new road had been built behind us, and a new subdivision would soon come and block the pristine view that we had enjoyed over the last two years. God was building a

---

1 (Jer. 33:3, NKJV)

new road for our lives, and we were thankful it was still in Michigan.

When I came home from work the next day, I mentioned to Jim I had not called the builder yet about the house we wanted to buy. That was the next step in faith for us to take. God had supplied us not only with a wonderful job for Jim but a salary that would allow us to purchase the home we wanted. I called the builder, reminded her who we were and that we had decided to buy the home we saw just a few weeks ago. She was very surprised I had called back because, in her experience, a lot of people say they are interested but they often do not follow through. However, there was a problem. Another person was interested in the house as well, and they were coming to put an offer on it in a few hours. I said, "We can be there in one hour!" Jim gave me his affirmative nod. I grabbed the checkbook, and we drove down to Michigan's great southwest to purchase our new home. As we were filling out the paperwork (fortunately, this was our seventh home, so we knew what we were doing), the other person that wanted to buy the house called on the builder's cell phone stating that he was delayed. He was a realtor and was hoping to purchase the home as an investment to turn around and sell after a period of time. Our builder then told him an offer had already been received on the house, and it was considered sold. He actually took it quite well and even asked if they had another house available. Case closed.

We found out our builder's policy was not to sell to the highest bidder but to the first buyer that offers them full price. We didn't know this. We just knew the house was worth the price, and we did not want to miss this opportunity. This new home was finished from top to bottom, and it was double the house that we previously had. God's word is true. He gave us double for our trouble again. With the relocation policy from Jim's new employer, we did not have to be concerned about our other home selling either. The relocation company would buy it at the appraised value if it did not sell in three months, and they would even advance us the equity in our current home for our down payment. This was almost too good to be true. The relocation agent assured us that Jim was working for a great company, and they did not want us to be concerned about these details. We were to get on with our lives so Jim could focus on his new job. *Oh my, this truly is a new season.* We signed the papers, and the home was ours. We wanted to live there for a long time, but we also knew it was a very good value; and if need be, we would do well if we sold again.

We shared with her some of our journey and how this home had been an answer to prayer and part of the restoration process in our lives. I hoped and prayed to live again in a small-town atmosphere as we did some fifteen years ago. Jim walked to work in that small town, and I wanted the good old days back. God was indeed restoring those years to us. Jim wanted to go back to a facility where he would have stability and input into the day-to-day operations and have authority over decisions being made. God was restoring that to us as well. It was hard to believe how fast everything was moving. Then the Lord reminded me of the vision of the sailboat and how quickly the storm had stopped, and the wind that tossed us to and fro was now, indeed, propelling us forward.

Our new home and the facility where Jim would be working were both in the enterprise zone. That meant our property taxes would be waived for a period of several years, and we would pay no state income tax because we lived and worked in this zone. Jim said, "I believe this is a land flowing with milk and honey!" I believed he was right!

When we were finished with the paperwork for our next home, we decided to drive by Jim's new office one more time. We stopped in front of the facility just in awe of all that God had done for us. Jim's new boss was still at work and looked out his window as we drove up. He came running out to greet us. I cannot tell you how that blessed us. I have always believed since we became Christians that you should be where you are celebrated, and Jim's boss made it perfectly clear this was a celebration. He invited us in for a chat. Jim and I had agreed to keep the purchase of the house quiet for a little while until we started the actual moving process, but within fifteen minutes into our conversation, Jim was so overjoyed that he could not keep silent about this awesome house that was within walking distance to the facility. Jim is not a chatty person, and he does not show his emotions often; but God was changing him from the inside out, and his heart was speaking now. It was awesome to see. His boss was delighted, and we all agreed the convenience would be very beneficial. During our conversation, we began to share briefly of our journey; and wouldn't you know it, his boss knew the area in Maine we almost moved to. In fact, he began to sing a little song about the chicken farms that caused the unbelievably obnoxious odor. To make it so much more fascinating, Jim's new boss and wife were actually from that very area in Maine. I am sure there are a lot of people who love the area, but it just did not love us. As we sat and enjoyed our conversation, Jim's boss asked us out to dinner with him and his wife. I almost cried; the Lord was showing us that this was a place where we could hang our hat and call home. *God, we are really here. You really have called us, and Jim really is employed by a great company and finally has a good boss. You are a good God.* We had a lovely dinner at the local club and drove home late that night, feeling like two young honeymooners who had been on the ride of their lives. Our heads were swimming. Our families hadn't even seen the house yet, and we could hardly wait to tell them our news. Jim had a job in West Michigan, and we just bought a brand-new house! It felt like we were starting our new life together all over again.

The next few weeks were filled with appointments of realtors, movers, and financial advisors. Jim started work right away, and I only had a few weeks left at the ministry center. I kept looking at the calendar and counted the days and months of our journey. I reviewed in my mind all the wonderful things God had told me and how they had, one by one, come true. But I could not get beyond the fact that the number seventeen came up several times. We had been unemployed seventeen months to the day when Jim started his new job. It was seventeen days from the first interview to the offer, and the difference in pay between Maine, the job he lost, and his new position were all in seventeen-thousand-dollar increments. I truly believed the number seventeen was significant because it just came up way too many times. God was letting us know beyond a shadow of a doubt that it was his mighty arm that worked this miracle in our lives. I called my sister, who studies biblical numerology, and found the definition of the number seventeen. It is victory. *Webster's New World Dictionary* defines *victory* as "the final and complete supremacy or superiority in battle, success in any contest or struggle involving the defeat of an opponent or the overcoming of obstacles." God says he will go before you and fight the battle, if we do the do and follow his principles. Deuteronomy 20:4 says, "For the lord your God is the one who goes with you to fight for you against your enemies to give you victory" (NIV).

Yes, God fights our battles, but we have the victory. The Lord had done an extraordinary thing in our lives. He has complete supremacy and is superior in battle. Through him, we have great success in any contest or struggle. Many people have gone through similar trials and suffering, and we need to learn from each other. The Lord has a plan and journey for each of us to walk through. If we listen to his voice, he will make our path straight and our way prosperous. We have a choice: do it God's way or our way. Truly, God has a better plan than we can imagine. God says in his word, "For I know the thoughts and plans that I have for you, says the Lord, thoughts and plans for welfare and peace and not for evil, to give you hope in your final outcome" (Jer. 29:11, TAB). He also says, "For as the heavens are higher than the earth, so are My ways higher than your ways, and My thoughts than your thoughts. says the lord" (Isa. 55:9, NKJV). *My goodness, that is so true.* Jim and I could not have imagined all the good that God had in store for us. We were willing to settle for a job that was so far away from what we wanted, but we trusted that God would direct our paths. We were willing, and maybe that is what the Lord was looking for—a willingness to obey even if it meant we would give up all that we had. I believe our Heavenly Father wants the very best for us; and in his loving goodness, mercy, and kindness, he has allowed us to live and abide here in Michigan's great southwest, close to those we love and cherish. But was this our final outcome?

Hindsight Diary 19

Though the Vision Tarry

Patience, patience, patience. Do not get ahead of God. He knows the times and the circumstances ahead. His vision is for eternity. His perspective is far above and ahead of you. I have always said his timing is perfect; he has lots of opportunities to be early, but he is never late. Do you remember a time when God came at 11:59:9? Write it down and thank him again for his marvelous timing.

God Knows the Plans and Paths of Your Life

Our new location was only an hour's drive from our sons and their families and our wonderful grandchildren, of which there were now two, Joshua *and* Naomi. We were still able to see our friends and visit our previous church whenever we wanted. The Lord caused us to prosper, and there was no sorrow. He filled us with his marvelous joy and began restoring us. There are always giants in the promised land but that's to be expected. Bigger levels, bigger devils, they say. But we have learned it is the Lord who will fight our battles. God is faithful. It is his desire to bless his children, but we must obey the word of God and do things his way.

As Jim and I filed our taxes from the previous year, I came across the budget that I had prepared back in December of 2003, when Jim first lost his job. I tucked it away in my monthly ledger and had totally forgotten about it. I had calculated Jim's severance pay, unemployment checks, noncompete compensation, along with my monthly income, together to see how long the money would last. I sat in amazement, staring at the figure at the bottom of the ledger sheet. I handed the paper to Jim, and we sat in silence in awe of God. After adding the income and subtracting the tithe, offerings, monthly payments, groceries, and other essentials, with a little cushion for life's daily surprises, the total months that I figured we would last before we had to sell our home came to *seventeen*. God says he knows our end from the beginning. He was guiding and directing our steps just as he promised he would. When Jim received the job offer, we were out of money—there was no more reserve; we were at the end.

The company that hired him not only paid for our relocation expenses, realtor and loan fees, house-hunting expenses, and move but also advanced us one month's salary upon the point of Jim's hire date as part of their company policy. When the Lord says he will meet our needs according to his riches in glory, he means it. When he says he will fight the battle and give us the victory, he means it.

A piece of paper slipped out of my Bible that I had forgotten about. Shortly after Jim lost his job, I remember crying out to the Lord, asking what I must do, or if I had done anything wrong for this calamity to have come upon us. His voice gently spoke to my heart, and I wrote it down and stuck it in my Bible. The Lord said to me, "This time of testing has not come for you to prove your love for me, but for *me* to prove my love for you."

Dearest saint, the Lord says, "Trust (lean on, rely on, and be confident) in the Lord and do good; so shall you dwell in the land and feed surely on His faithfulness, and truly you shall be fed" (Ps. 37:3, TAB). It may not be the path that you would have chosen, but if you truly allow him to lead you, your life will be blessed far more than you could have ever hoped or dreamed. That little note with God's message for me was dated exactly seventeen days from the date Jim lost his job. The Lord was talking to me all the way through our journey. I was learning to listen to his voice and not the roar of the lions. We declared God's word that says, "Thanks be to God, who gives us the victory [making us conquerors] through our Lord Jesus Christ" (1 Cor. 15:57, TAB).

Hindsight Diary 20

God Knows the Plan and Paths of Your Life

The Lord has a plan for your life. He knew you before you were born and his thoughts toward you are, "for welfare and peace and not for evil, to give you hope in your final outcome" (Jer. 29:11, TAB) and "[taking paths which He prepared ahead of time], that we should walk in them [living the good life which He prearranged and made ready for us to live]" (Eph. 2:10, TAB). Note there are paths for you to follow, which means someone has gone there before you. You do not have to go alone, nor do you have to chart unknown territory. They say the way you start a journey is by taking the first step. What would that first step be?

It Ain't Over till It's Over, and It Ain't Over Yet!

You may have thought this story was over. Well, I did too. However, the adventure continued. We have had some challenges. My health was attacked in a vicious way—another giant in the land to overcome. The enemy tried to bring on an autoimmune disease against my body. I noticed some strange symptoms like easy bruising and little red dots on my feet and ankles. I knew something was not right, so I sought wisdom and knowledge. The Bible says to seek after wisdom. Wisdom said, "Go to the doctor." I researched my symptoms on the Internet, and the doctor confirmed that I was fighting ITP (idiopathic thrombocytopenic purpura). My blood platelets were diminishing because my body's antibodies had turned against me and was attacking my platelets. You need your platelets to clot your blood, so if you get cut or poked, you will not bleed to death. My doctor was slightly concerned, so he sent me to the lab for blood work. I had the blood drawn on a Friday morning, and by two o'clock that same day, I was with a hematologist in the hospital, getting prepped for a transfusion of platelets. The acceptable count for platelets is 140 thousand. A year ago, my platelet count was 331 thousand, but on that Friday, I had only eight thousand little platelets trying to do their job.

It was a scary situation, but I was not afraid. In fact, I felt more inconvenienced about the whole event. The doctor said that I had to be watched the whole time. If I fell and bumped my head or have any other injury, I could bleed to death before they could patch me up. So I obeyed the doctors and spent my weekend enjoying the hospitality of our local hospital. That weekend, Jim and I had plans for our children and grandchildren to come down for my birthday. Needless to say, our plans changed, but our two sons came down anyway to see Mom and find out what the heck was going on. They walked in with their father that Friday evening, and they looked to me like huge, angelic linebackers. Honestly, when the three of them walked through the door, I thought I saw the enemy jump out the window. I felt so safe when they prayed for me and took authority over the situation.

The Lord showed me a brief description of what was happening at—you guessed it—3:33 a.m. while lying on my hospital bed. I had taken a hit from the enemy, and the Lord used an example of a football game. He explained it to me like this: the red blood cells represented the defensive line, and the white blood cells were the offensive line. The platelets were the cheerleaders. Well, you know what it's like when the cheerleaders are down in front and they are leading a cheer to help the team. They turn to the fan base to get them to cheer for the team. Usually, only a few fans do. They are too busy watching the game, and they forget to cheer for the team with the direction of the cheerleaders. Well, that's what happened to me. The cheerleaders were tired. They had been cheering the team on for a long time, and they were worn out. The Lord showed me how I had been encouraging everyone around me, but I didn't let my fan base know I was tired and needed their encouragement. It was time to call in the prayer warriors and kick butt. I realized that's why my sons and husband looked so much like linebackers when they came into my room. They took the ball away from the devil and kicked him out the window. When I left the hospital, my platelet count rose up to fifty thousand. The doctor put me on steroids to help bulk up what platelets I did have until they replenished themselves. I felt perfectly well when I went to the hospital. Even after the transfusion I felt fine, but when they put me on the steroids—well, that was a different story. Weekly, I would have to have my blood drawn to check the counts, but weekly, my platelets continued to drop again. They increased the dosage of the steroids and with that came all the side effects: weight gain, bloated face and body, the shakes, sleeplessness, and I felt on edge all the time. And to top it off, the doctors really didn't know how to treat it, much less figure out why I had this ITP in the first place.

Jim and I went to the great physician, Jesus Christ. The word of God said, "By His stripes we are healed" (Isa. 53:5, NKJV). But why was I not seeing the manifestation? I began to lose heart. Then my youngest son, Matt, reminded—actually, more scolded—me that God meant what he said and I would be healed completely and not to settle for anything less. *Well, yes and amen*, I thought. The whole family really stood in the gap for me and prayed for my complete restoration. I began to do research to find out what this ITP was. I came across several Web sites and individuals who were experiencing this rare disorder. Through my research, I found information on a natural way to strengthen my own immune system. I knew I had to be proactive regarding my health, so I ordered the natural supplements and continued to pray and believe the Lord was my healer. I stood on God's word that said I was healed of all infirmities. I listened daily to scriptures on CD and fed my spirit with the word of God. After taking large doses of steroids and the natural supplements, the platelets that had fallen below twenty thousand slowly began to rise again. The physical symptoms of the steroids were really taking their toll, but I knew that I was being healed and continued on. While on the medication, I did not even look like myself. This puffy, buggy-eyed girl looking back at me in the mirror made me cry, and I had to fight the fear and the lies of the enemy that kept whispering in my ears. "You will always look like this," he would sneer. The shakes were unbelievable, the constant state of confusion and sleepless nights were a nightmare, but I trusted in God's word and the prayers of family and friends for my total healing. As the platelets stared to increase, the doctor slowly started decreasing the steroids. Within one month of taking the supplements, my platelet count started doubling. When I went to the doctor for my checkup, all he could do was scratch his head. He had never seen platelets go from such a low count to a steady triple-digit. That opened up a door of opportunity to tell him about the Lord, prayer, and the supplements I was taking. I think he is *still* trying to figure it out. Today, my healing has manifested itself completely. I am medication-free, and my platelets are at a steady 333 thousand, my favorite number.

I do not want anyone to think that just because you get to your land of promise, it is easy street from there on. Remember, the giants lived in the promised land. You must keep doing what you did to get to where you are, because there will always be battles. We had to battle with a few giants that year, but none quite as big as the next one to come.

Jim's job had been going well; the facility had not been making as much money as they had hoped, but with a little more time, they should be able to turn the corner and get to where they wanted to be. My health was improving daily, and my strength slowly renewed.

My phone rang at 7:55 a.m. on August 30, 2006. It was Jim calling from work, but the caller ID said he was calling from his cell phone and not his office. His voice had an eerie, familiar tone to it and sounded tight and constricted. I could tell he was standing outside and speaking softly so as not to be heard. We knew one of the new VPs of the company was touring the facility that day, and I was very surprised that Jim was calling me at that time of the morning. Within moments, I knew this day and our life had taken yet another turn. The new VP planned to come in and have a look over this small operation in Michigan's great southwest. He came in at six o'clock in the morning to speak with the night shift that was leaving and first shift that would be arriving. By six thirty that morning, they shut down the plant and let everyone go, everyone except Jim.

The blood of Jesus has never lost its power. His faithfulness endures forever. Oh my, it felt like we were once again at the top of the employment roller coaster and just getting ready for the descent. We were so grateful for continued employment, but there were lots of questions and no answers. For now, Jim was to help with the orderly shutdown of the facility. His boss, office staff, and all facility workers were gone. The company had given them severance packages and employment assistance, but their time at that plant was done that morning. They retained a few temporary maintenance people to help with the shutdown, but the doors were closed and contracts cancelled. It was over. Jim and I were in shock. A million things rolled through our minds. *Why?* came up a lot. *Why were we spared? Why now? Why do we have to move and, worse yet, where? This is our promised land, God. Why?*

We both remembered the relocation question asked during Jim's interviews. Well, of course we would consider relocation if need be. We wanted the job. However, we really did not give it a second thought after that. After all, we were in Michigan, and that was all the mattered.

The doors of our lives in West Michigan were closing. The grief was knocking at my heart, fear was running toward me, and the lions were roaring in my ears again; lies, lies, lies they screamed. "God has left you, he has lied to you and you will lose it all." I could feel their hot breath on the back of my neck. The devil was trying to take my focus off God's promises and focus on his lies. I did the only thing I knew to do. I grabbed my Bible and spoke God's words out loud at the top of my lungs, "I will say of the Lord, He is my Refuge and my Fortress, my God; on

Him I lean and rely, and in Him I [confidently] trust!...A thousand may fall at your side, and ten thousand at your right hand, but it shall not come near you. Only a spectator shall you be [yourself inaccessible in the secret place of the Most High]" (Ps. 91:2,7,8, TAB).

I cried. I did not want to leave my new home, I did not want to start all over again, and I did not want to be far away from my family. *Lord, you promised me it would never be that hard again.* Then I heard his still small voice, "Jim still has a job, doesn't he?"

When they closed the facility that fateful day on August 30, the vice president said they valued Jim and felt there was a place for him within the larger organization. Jim's position would evolve as they restructured and redefined their role in the marketplace. The facility in West Michigan was just losing too much money for it to be viable. Hard decisions had to be made. For now, Jim's role was fuzzy. He was to help with the shutdown, which meant calling suppliers and environmental agencies to help with the cleanup and orderly closure. Thankfully, he would continue to work with the other facility in Tennessee that depended on him for his technical expertise, but it was over for us at this location, on the southwest corner of our Mitten.

We were in shock but not completely surprised. We received a letter at the beginning of the year that said it would be a transitional year for the company. There was movement within the upper-level management. Jim identified words in the notice that brought up some red flags. *Realignment* and *redirecting*, terminology that usually meant big changes for everyone. The company said it wanted to keep us on but was not sure where.

There were several facilities, and they said they did not want us to move twice, whatever that meant. So for two months, we knew we would be leaving Michigan, but we had no idea where. Our lives went on hold. These were sad days for Jim. So many questions, but answers were few in coming. Jim was the last person hired and the only one left. It reminded us of the scripture, "So the last will be first, and the first last" (Matt. 20:16, NKJV). Strange events, but we chose to trust God on this different path he was leading us on. The Bible does say *paths* for us to follow for the good life. We knew the Lord had a plan for us, but I cried daily. Just the thought of leaving Michigan was almost too much to bear. We loved the state, the people, and our families. Why would God make us move after keeping us in West Michigan? The Lord was requiring obedience again, and we've learned to be obedient the hard way.

Jim and I decided to be with our family as much as possible during those months. We knew we would be leaving soon, and we were determined to make the most of the time we had left. As we would share our story with our friends back at our old church, they would encourage us with the story of Abraham. Every time it seemed I turned on the TV, the evangelists would be talking about Abraham's journey to Egypt. We even met some people at church who were moving away, and they spoke of Abraham and how they had to move away from their family and friends too. Employment was drying up in Michigan. A famine was coming upon the land.

It was finally decided our next home would be in South Carolina. It was the best of all the possible locations, except of course Michigan. This was the biggest facility in the company and one of the largest in North America—the mother ship, so to speak. We would be small fish in a very large pond, but employed fish.

The company again would take care of everything, just like the first time. We were assigned a relocation agent, and all we had to do was find another home to call our own—again. This would make three houses in four years. I did not want to move away from my kids and grandkids, friends and family, and all that felt comfortable and secure. I suppressed those thoughts and feelings, but like little bubbles underwater, they would come to the surface and pop. No matter how I tried to keep them from floating up, they would bubble up from some deep well, like air needing to escape. *No, God, I do not want to leave home.* It was harder to be obedient this time.

Our families were happy for us. They saw the greater picture and were delighted that there was a warm spot to visit during Michigan's long cold winters. They went through the valley with us during Jim's long months of unemployment, and we knew they would have a hard time if we turned this opportunity down. We knew the sacrifice we were making, and honestly, we just did not want to move or start over again. However, I knew in my heart if I could just see the area and feel God's presence there, we would be all right. Jim and I both had to fight the raging battle in our minds. We made a decision based on God's word that says, "Casting down arguments and every high thing that exalts itself against the knowledge of God, bringing every thought into captivity to the obedience of Christ" (2 Cor. 10:5, NKJV).

It is hard to hold every thought captive when the enemy is quick with his lies, but we chose to fight this fight by using Jesus's example. "It is written, 'Man shall not live by bread alone, but by every word that proceeds from the mouth of God'" (Matt. 4:4, NKJV). We spoke God's words, not ours.

It appears to me as I write about our journey that this story seems like such a downer. Well, I guess I would rather be truthful than to tell everyone it was butterflies and roses. Walking the walk of faith is not easy. It is rewarding, if you faint not, but not easy either. I think many Christians think that when life gets tough, God must have abandoned them, or they have done something wrong to bring this upon them. I used to think that way too. But the reality is life can be hard. We live in a broken world, and there will always be things to deal with. However, if you choose to follow God's principles, even the hardest day of our lives is like the best day for a person who does not know God. The Lord is our source, and he will meet our needs, but we must do the deed. We must work the word of God for the word of God to work. That means trusting even when you do not see anything happening, speaking what God says about you even when you don't see the plan. It's like planting a seed and waiting for the new growth. It takes time. The seed is under the soil where you can't see it, but you have to trust it is growing. Then at just the right time, its little head will appear, seed, time, and then harvest.

We knew now we would be moving outside of Michigan and most likely move over the holidays. Fortunately, I did my Christmas shopping well in advance. I was so thankful we could once again buy presents for our families. I wrapped the gifts and took them to a central place in Grand Rapids where I knew the majority of our family would be. I knew this move would mess up our holiday, but I did not want it to interfere with our families' plans.

I spent hours daily researching on the Internet, looking at homes in all the possible locations they may move us to. This way we would be prepared when we were given the final location where they wanted Jim to report for duty. I knew as soon as we got the news we would have to hit the ground running, and run we did. It was decided Jim would start work the first day of January at the large facility in South Carolina, so right after Thanksgiving, Jim and I flew down to find our new home in the Carolinas. This was a completely different experience than when we went to Maine. I had never been to South Carolina but was excited to see what everyone was talking about. It was lovely and warm. The people were very friendly and courteous, and fortunately, I did advance house hunting via the Internet, so it went very smoothly. So well, in fact, that the first house we saw we loved and eventually bought. After comparing several other homes to the first one we looked at, we knew which house was the one for us in this next season. However, before making the offer, Jim and I went back to our hotel room and prayed. "If Your Presence does not go with us, do not bring us up from here" (Exod. 33:15, NKJV). Jim and I took time to sit in God's presence. This was a huge decision and commitment, and we did not want to make any mistakes. We felt the Lord's peace, and this was where we were to live for now. We had what we needed to go forward. So we drove to the real estate office and made an offer on our eighth home.

Before leaving on our house hunting trip to South Carolina, the Lord gave me housing criteria for our next home, and this house fit the bill perfectly. Number one, the house must be in the right location. Good for Jim's commute and good for me for shopping and necessities. Number two, the house must be big enough. You can make a big house small, but not a small house big. And number three, it must be the right price for our budget; we were not to overextend ourselves. The house that we bought met every condition out of the twenty houses we looked at. In fact, it had every detail that we needed in the perfect house, and it was the only one that fit the bill. We believed this was a God thing. I knew when we saw our new home we could do this, and we did. Believing is seeing, and seeing *is* believing. The house was 90 percent complete, so we had the privilege of working with the builder the rest of the week, picking out tile for the kitchen and hardware and other items that we wanted. We really liked the house. I told the builder I felt he built it just for us.

Now, you might be saying that I'm putting too much value into a house. Well, I was concerned about that too. I do not worship a house; after all, they are just brick and wood. So I checked my heart and asked God why homes are so important to me. He began to show me that during my childhood, I did not have a place to call home. Every time we moved—and it was often—I would try and make it my home, but we never stayed long. God was healing those memories by showing me home is where your heart is. And my heart is with the Lord and my husband. Each home the Lord has given Jim and me filled a void, and each home fulfilled a need in our lives. The good news is I'm able to let go of those homes and launch out with conviction when the next house comes on the horizon. So this will be my home for as long as God chooses it to be. No earthly house will ever be our home forever anyway. We are foreigners in this land—ambassadors, so to speak. Heaven is our home, and we are here only until our assignment is over, which means it is South Carolina for now.

As I watched the movers drive the big orange truck away with all of our worldly possessions heading toward the Carolinas, the Lord spoke softly to my heart and said, "If you will do this, I will do that." Tears filled my eyes. *Yes, Lord, I'll do this for you, even if I do not know what that "that" is.*

Hindsight Diary 21

It Ain't Over till It's Over, and It Ain't Over Yet

"And they overcame him by the blood of the Lamb and by the word of their testimony" (Rev. 12:11, NKJV). We are to overcome, but it is a journey of prevailing. Every day we will have choices to make. Those choices will chart the course of your life. The word of God says, "Death and life are in the power of the tongue, and they who indulge in it shall eat the fruit of it [for death or life]" (Prov. 18:21, TAB). It all comes down to this: What does faith say? What words are you speaking? Write down some positive affirmations from God's word for your current situation.

A New Chapter

The trip down to South Carolina was a new adventure and chapter in our lives.

Things were definitely different down south. Never in a million years did I ever think we would be living south of the Michigan border again. The weather was a big change. We were used to the four seasons and variations of weather patterns. There just isn't much change in South Carolina—nice and sunny most of the time. Somehow, we would manage. Southern folk are incredibly friendly, almost uncomfortably so for us Midwesterners. We Northerners have this space issue—I'll stay in mine and you stay in yours. I never realized what an independent lot we were until we moved down south. When they say, "Hey, how y'all doing?" They really want to know how you are doing! They expect a response. Jim and I would fumble over our words, but after a while, we were able to converse in a more hospitable manner other than saying, "Just fine." Now it's, "Doing fine. How y'all doing?" and then another conversation would transpire. We had to really work on our own Southern hospitality.

It took Jim a while to find his spot in the huge paper mill down south. He balanced his job in South Carolina with his continued responsibilities in Tennessee, thanking God for his continued provision.

It did not take to long to unpack and get established. We were actually getting pretty good at it. As we continued to believe God for his favor, we slowly began to feel more comfortable with our lives down south. The Lord spoke to my heart one day while taking a walk. He said for Jim and me to be comfortable here but not content. Comfortable was temporary, contentment was permanent. We were to affect the culture and not let it affect us. You see, it's all about our assignment: the call of God on our lives. No matter where we live, we are to affect the atmosphere around us. When the Israelites were taken captive to Babylon, the Lord told them to plant, settle, marry, and be a part of the plan. But God did not say for them to become part of the culture. When it came time for their ultimate release, only 2 percent of the Israelites left. Instead of affecting the culture, the culture affected them. This is not to say we are in any way better or above those whom we are around. However, we are to be ambassadors for Christ. It is Christ in us, the hope of glory.

We missed our families, but we were determined to learn as much as we could from this experience. We found a dynamic church that stretched us in very good ways, and the Lord's favor was present. We were able to return to Michigan often and fortunately did not miss many special occasions. In fact, we had several visits from family members to the Allen's Southern Retreat.

After several months of writing on this book and setting up housekeeping, I thought it would be a good time to return to the workforce. The interviews began, and I was hired quickly as an executive assistant to a CFO of a technology company. It was a great opportunity, and, as Jim put it, "I got my edge back." I didn't know I had lost it, but thankfully, it's back, for whatever that's worth. It was a great position, and I made some lifelong friends. But after seven months of work, I began to feel a longing in my spirit to finish this book. The Lord was tugging at my heartstrings and started showing me the people that have been downsized and their great need for encouragement. It was time for me to return to the sanctuary of my home office and complete my assignment. Then I remembered a dream I had several years ago when this story first began.

In my dream, I was a little girl walking down a dirt road. I had on a pair of dungarees that had lots of pockets. I was walking down this road humming and singing and picking up precious stones and treasures along the way. Then I heard my name being called. "Cindy, Cindy, come home." I stopped what I was doing and ran as fast as I could. I flew up the stairs and laid all my precious treasures out on the bed, but upon looking at them, I noticed they were just ordinary sticks and stones. I woke up and asked the Lord what the dream was about. He said all those precious objects were just that, earthly treasures—things I thought were important but, upon second glance, just sticks and stones. Then he said, "But you always come when you're called."

The Lord was calling me again. I love to hear my Father's voice. Obeying is not an option. It is hard at times to lay down my wants and my desires; however, God's ways are so much better. It was time to leave my job and follow after the voice of God. He allowed me a season to get my edge back and collect what I thought were precious treasures, but when it comes down to serving him, he knows I will come when I'm called. I turned in my notice at work and was quickly replaced by someone who would take the position to another level.

We are now at the end of our seven-year cycle of employment, unemployment, and reemployment. It has truly been a fight of faith. This is not where Jim and I plan to stay, but it is God's protection in the storm of unemployment—our safe harbor. For many, the employment outlook has been cruel. However, if you listen to the voice of the Lord, he will direct your path. I guarantee it *will* be a path of unknowns and ups and downs, but the Lord promises it will be a path for the good life. Ephesians 2:10 says, "For we are God's [own] handiwork (His workmanship), recreated in Christ Jesus, [born anew] that we may do those good works which God predestined (planned beforehand) for us [taking paths which He prepared ahead of time], that we should walk in them [living the good life which He prearranged and made ready for us to live]" (TAB).

I have no idea how God will move us back home, but that's not my concern. I am to cast my cares and concerns upon him because I can trust him. I love the way the Message Bible translates Jeremiah 29:11, "I'll show up and take care of you as I promised and bring you back home. I know what I'm doing. I have it all planned out—plans to take care of you, not abandon you, plans to give you the future you hope for." I've written this book in hindsight. You know what they say, hindsight is 20/20. Most lessons are learned that way, looking back on what you did right and what you did wrong. Somewhat like driving up a steep mountain. In order to reach the summit, you have to take switchbacks. They are narrow roads up a mountain trail that switch back and forth to help you climb upward at a safe and slow rate. When you reach the summit and look down, your perspective is so different from when you were down at the bottom looking up.

I'm sure there are things Jim and I could have or should have done differently, but when you are in the middle of the switchback, usually your option is to go forward or off the road down the cliff. We knew that God would do his part if we did ours. I've said to Jim many times that I'm amazed how the Lord took a man who hates to move, put him with a woman that has security issues, and then moves them about the country, causing them not only to move often but to be totally dependent on him. It makes for an incredible journey.

Hindsight Diary 22

A New Chapter

Never let go of the promises of God. Never. They are yes and amen. God's final word on it is, "For the vision is yet for an appointed time and it hastens to the end [fulfillment]; it will not deceive or disappoint. Though it tarry, wait [earnestly] for it, because it will surely come; it will not be behindhand on its appointed day" (Hab. 2:3, TAB). It will surely come! How will your story end?

Epilogue

How do you know when a story is over?

What is the difference between a last chapter and a new beginning?

This was my dilemma; is it the beginning of a new book or the last chapter of *I Thought I Heard the Lion's Roar?* The definition of *epilogue* is a chapter at the end that serves as a comment or conclusion to bring closure. Yes, this is indeed an epilogue, for it brings closure to an amazing story of God's faithfulness to his word and the work of his hands.

Jim and I spent seven long years in South Carolina. We hoped to live away from our family and our precious Mitten State for only a few years. However, as hard as we tried to move, we were stuck. Jim had many interviews over those seven years with viable companies in or near Michigan, but those opportunities always seemed to fall through. They would either say Jim had a great resume, but it was the wrong fit or he had "too much horsepower," which usually meant he was too old. In our minds we were only in our forties and fifties, but once you added up the experience on the resume, the numbers said Jim was definitely in his sixties, and too close to retirement for them to take a chance. Retirement? That was years away for us! We weren't ready, and we didn't have enough money in the old 401(k) to last for our expected life spans. So what do you do during those times of frustration? I thought about throwing a pity party, but of course no one would come. Or we could stay home and pout and get mad at God and each other, but that didn't help either. So Jim and I did the only thing we knew to do: follow Ephesians 6:8, help make happen for others what we want God to make happen for us. Cindy's translation.

January 15, 2010

Very often the Lord speaks to me in riddles. The Bible says, "It is the glory of God to conceal a thing, but the glory of kings is to search a thing out" (Prov. 25:2 TAB) On January 15, 2010, I was about to search out a thing. That day while beseeching the Lord in prayer regarding our extended stay in South Carolina, I heard this riddle in my heart, "Would you be willing to stay a little longer if you could stay forever where you want?" It was so clear and concise I knew it was His voice, the voice of God. I wrote down the riddle before I forgot and pondered on it. What does "a little longer" mean? A day in the Lord is like a thousand years…And truly I have no idea where I want to stay forever other than somewhere back home in Michigan. It's a big state, and it actually has two parts, upper and lower peninsula. I knew I just wanted to be somewhere on the Mitten, and I figured most likely in a paper mill town where Jim could continue to work until we retire. This was a mystery to me, so I tucked the piece of paper away in my Bible for further contemplation. "A little longer?"

While waiting for my "little longer," we decided it would be better to be more involved in our church and community. We were always involved in every church we attended, so we thought no time like the present to volunteer again. Of course in doing this, we made new friends, helped others, advanced the gospel, and were even privileged to help with a new church plant. By helping others, we took our eyes off ourselves and actually started to enjoy life down South. And for fun, we took advantage of Jim's love of Ford Mustangs and got involved in the Carolina Mustang Club, where we found more new friends, traveled to wonderful places in the Carolinas, and helped with fund-raising activities for different charities.

While in South Carolina, I worked a couple of jobs, but the only position that was my best fit came through a series of interesting circumstances. We were attending a church plant in SC that was part of a much larger church in the Charlotte area. This local church met in a movie theater, which meant they had to set up and take down every Sunday. At that time, I was working as an executive assistant to the president of a television network ministry but decided I wanted to be more involved with something local. One Sunday during worship, I said to God that I wanted to help the small growing church we attended, and if it was His will, would He please open a door for me? Later that day, I mentioned to Jim my conversation with God during worship. Upon mentioning that, he proceeded to hand me the morning's bulletin. Apparently, the large church in Charlotte was looking for an administrative assistant for the pastor of discipleship. Well, I guess that was as close to a sign as I could get, so I applied; and after several interviews, I was hired to work at the main church in Charlotte. This was not quite what I asked for as I really didn't want to travel to Charlotte on a daily basis with all the traffic, but I trusted that if God had opened this door, I could trust him with all the details. Almost every position I have worked (and there have been many) I find that I am usually assigned to a person. I knew when I met the discipleship pastor in my interview he would be the next person I would be serving in this next season. Mike (my new boss) was one of the nicest people I have ever met but also one of the most unorganized. He would be my assignment, and I would help make happen for him what I wanted God to make happen for me. However, I was still very interested in serving the church plant we attended at the theater, but this was my job for now. Amazingly enough, within the first week of my employment, as we were deciding how to order my daily responsibilities, my new boss and HR director asked if I would be willing to cut some hours from my week with him to help the smaller church plant at the theater! God's fingerprints were all over this. My new catchphrase for that season was "I'm not driving the bus." If I would just trust that God had my best in mind and relaxed, I could sit back and let my Heavenly Father drive the bus! My days were spent doing what I do best: keeping my boss organized and working alongside others with like goals and beliefs. As the year progressed, we fell into a good rhythm, and my time with Mike and helping the church plant was indeed a great fit. But the funny thing about a good rhythm, something always comes along that changes. Activities were picking up at the large church, and the church plant was growing like crazy, so my carved-out time for the church plant began taking a deeper cut into my workday. The church decided it was time to raise funds to move the church plant from a theater to their own building. This is a debt-free church, so until the funds were available, we continued on with hope for our own space in the near future. The community really caught the vision and raised the funds quickly to purchase and refit a large building just down the road. After seven long years in the theater of setting up and tearing down every Sunday, they would have their own place to worship, and I would be moving with them to full-time. It was a difficult decision to leave my boss in Charlotte. We had developed a trust that was unique and special, but we decided, for the greater good, it was time for me to move with the church plant and continue to follow God's leading. There was much to do with this new building, but we had a wonderful band of volunteers and staff that helped make a large task doable. Our first service would be mid-December. We decided to do what they call a soft launch. No advertising, just letting our 350-member congregation ease into their new location. We prepared for double the amount of attendees for our first service due to word of mouth and estimated around six to seven hundred folks with families and friends. The new facility would fit just under one thousand, so we had plenty of room to grow. We planned on one service for the first few months, giving us time to adjust to our new digs. The volunteers and staff had worked hard for the past seven years setting up and tearing down every Sunday, and now finally, everything would be set up permanently; so all we had to do was to arrive, stand at our posts, and welcome the folks into our new place of worship. And arrive they did. Do you remember the movie *Field of Dreams*—"If you build it, he will come"? Well, that is what I thought when one of our volunteers came to me with tears in her eyes on our first morning. She said there were hundreds of cars lined up and down the road trying to get into the parking lot. They were coming in droves. We had to bring in more chairs, and folks were seated in the foyer watching the service on our big jumbo screens broadcasting to the overflow. This was all God, and he had certainly blown away all our preconceived notions. So much for our plans to wait a few months to go to two services. Apparently, God had other plans. As you can only imagine, our staff meeting the next week was a time of great joy and enormous humility. We knew we had nothing to do with this marvelous act of God. He was large and in charge.

I loved my job. I was now in full-time ministry at my own church and only minutes from home. Everything was just about perfect for me. Unfortunately, not for my Jimbob. His life at work just didn't get better; in fact, it got worse. His job at the mill had changed over the past seven years, and not in a good way. His responsibilities increased significantly and moved him into supervision away from the technical and analytical tasks he enjoyed as well as adding additional work hours to his already ten-hour days with no extra compensation. It was the new normal. In fact, the company struggled through a merger and bankruptcy, so he had to actually take a cut in pay while working more hours. These were times that really tested his resolve. Jim's drive to look for another job was still strong, but the constant rejections were tiring and difficult. However, just when I'd think we should give up looking for a job in Michigan and try to make a go for it in the South, at least until Jim could retire, I'd hear the scripture from Luke 18:1–8 either in my heart or someone would preach on it. Luke 18 is about the parable of the widow that would not give up. She so pestered the Judge that he finally gave up and said, "Because this widow continues to bother me, I will defend and protect and avenge her; lest she give me intolerable annoyance and wear me out by her continual coming or at the last she come and rail on me, or assault me or strangle me. Then the Lord said, *Listen* to what the unjust judge says! And will not our just God defend and protect and avenge His elect, His chosen ones, who cry to Him day and night? Will He defer them and delay help on their behalf? I tell you, He will defend and protect and avenge them speedily. However, when the Son of man comes will He find persistence in the faith on the earth?" (TAB).

The whole theme of this book is on discerning the voice of God. The key word in the above parable is *listen*. There are so many distractions in our world making so much noise that often we are unable to hear God's voice. This is why it is so important to read God's Word. Very often he will speak to you while reading, or the word of God will calm and settle you down enough to hear him speaking to you. Also when you read the Bible, you are literally building a relationship with the Lord. You are learning about his principles and way of doing things. Just like your parents taught you their principles. Establishing a relationship with God is a lot like establishing a relationship with anyone—the more time you spend together, the more you recognize their voice. Then you will be able to discern his voice amongst all the other voices. "And your ears will hear a word behind you, saying, This is the way; walk in it, when you turn to the right hand and when you turn to the left" (Isa. 30:21, TAB)

I learned that my walk with God is about knowing his word and listening with persistence in faith. Did I truly believe and trust that God would rescue us and bring us back home? Yes, I did, I just didn't know all the details. Again, I wasn't driving the bus.

During the next few years, we continued to look for ways to get back home while making our long drive back to Michigan several times a year. But we were determined to make every effort to enjoy our time in the Carolinas as well. By now we developed some great friendships, and even though our hearts longed to be home, our bodies were still very much in the South.

The Christmas of 2012 became a game changer. We were involved in an interesting interview process that could take us to the Upper Peninsula (UP) of Michigan in what seemed like a perfect fit for Jim as a technical manager. We had always loved the UP with its remoteness and clean air. It would not be as close to family as I wanted but would still be in the boundaries of Michigan, and half the drive for family visits. Interview plans were made to fly to the UP after the holidays. We were so hopeful this opportunity would be our ticket closer to home.

During that Christmas holiday came the hard reality that our folks were getting older and we would need to be much closer to them very soon. Jim's mother's health over the past six months had taken its toll, and we were facing some big decisions regarding her care. It appeared she was slipping away mentally, and we were distressed that we weren't close by to help with her care and that of my folks as well. While on the return flight home from the UP after the interviews, we were sitting on the tarmac in Detroit, getting ready to change plans. I heard God say very clearly three things. So clearly that I wrote them down: (1) Long approach, (2) Course correction, (3) Final destination. I had no idea what that meant, but once again, God had given me another riddle. I was still working on the "Would you be willing to stay a little longer if you could stay forever where you want?" puzzle! Revelation was about to come!

Well unfortunately, just like all the other job opportunities we had pursued, this one faded as well. They hired internally—rats, they could have saved us the effort!

We did have a good trip up to the UP though and even found a nifty house on Lake Michigan that would have been great, but just like the others, we had hope for the holidays then disappointment a month later. But something happened that surprised Jim and me both with the disappointing news. We really weren't *that* disappointed. We both had this overriding peace, and knowing that we were definitely moving this time, we just didn't know where. There was a deep-down conviction that there was going to be a happy ending to this journey, and the ending was coming sooner than later. Our concerns for our elderly parents were genuine, and we believed it was time to move back home to Michigan to help with their care, but we really didn't know how that would be possible. Course correction?

At first we thought about moving in with the folks to care for them, but after running that idea up the flag pole, we decided they weren't ready for that drastic of a move—and frankly, neither were we, but we were willing. Our concerns for their well-being began to override our own personal desires to move back to Michigan and became more about taking care of our parents and their needs. In our prayers, we asked God to show himself and his will for us. We were constantly checking our motives to make sure this wasn't about what we wanted but about what God wanted. Then one Sunday, Jim and I made the decision to look closely at our finances and to see if there was affordable housing close to both of our folks in Northern Michigan. After crunching the numbers and looking at housing online, we were very pleasantly surprised that there indeed just might be a way back home we had not considered.

You see, all this time, we hoped God would move us back the same way he always moved in our lives: get Jim a job then the company would move us, pay the moving expenses, and we would live happily ever after back in our Mitten State, because that has usually been the pattern in the past. But we were entering into a new season. Interestingly enough, when we moved down to South Carolina, I was very conservative with the relocation money the company gave us and put it in our savings account to never touch. I had a feeling we may need that money to pay for the big orange truck packed full of our belongings for the move back home. Sometimes, its good to pay attention to those feelings.

We decided, in order to meet the needs of both sets of parents, it would be better to live closer to them than to our children and grandchildren. I confided with one of my pastoral friends about the change in my heart and how surprised I was that I had this overriding feeling to put our parents at a higher priority. She reminded me it was the call of Christ on our lives and to not be surprised at what other changes may be in store for us.

I believe that only God can change a heart, and he was really doing a number on Jim and me. Our motive had changed from "Just get us back home, God, to "We need to be home to take care of our parents." Very often when the motive is right, things begin to fall into place. And the biggest surprise of all was that place was back in Traverse City, Michigan, where it all began. We never thought we would move back to TC. It isn't a paper mill town; it's just too nice, too lovely, too much for us to hope for. But a beautiful window had opened, and the cool breezes of the Grand Traverse Bay began to beckon us back home.

When it actually looked like we could find adequate housing, we decided to drive the sixteen hours north again to look for our new home. It was an amazing five days. We drove up on a Wednesday, looked at some condos Thursday, made an offer on Friday, which was accepted on Saturday, spent Mother's Day with both mothers and our two daughter-in-laws and drove back to South Carolina on Sunday with a signed purchase agreement in our hands. We took the first step, expecting God to show us the next step in this awesome move of faith. Some of our friends wondered why we just didn't quit our jobs and move up and find a place, but we knew we would have to continue to work a few more months in the South while we financed the condo and sold our current home. After all, what mortgager is going to lend us money to buy a second home without a good monthly income coming in. But this was the beginning of the end in South Carolina, and God was guiding and directing our footsteps on this pathway back home. My anchor scripture for the past several years continually came to my mind: "I'll show up and take care of you as I promised and bring you back home. I know what I'm doing. I have it all planned out—plans to take care of you, not abandon you, plans to give you the future you hope for" (Jer. 29:11, Message Bible).

Bring me back home? Seriously, my life has taken so many twists and turns, I really never called anyplace home. Where was home? Through all the moves as a child and my adult life, I always wondered where *home* was. In fact, I would often call it this "noise in my head" like a white noise that took the form of a constant question of where is home? I knew Michigan was home, and I would be content with any place on the Mitten. But our God is a very specific God. If you ever doubted his specificity, just look at the flowers or bark on trees or the hairs on you arm. God is way into the details of everything. So why should I be surprised that he is into all the details of my life as well? Traverse City was the most logical place to relocate to help with our parents. It was a thirty-minute drive to Jim's folks in Northport and a twenty-minute drive the opposite direction to my folks in Williamsburg. Traverse is pretty much in the middle, not to mention a quick two-and-a-half-hour drive south to see our children in Grand Rapids. This is working out perfectly, and we found just the right condo to accommodate our needs. Now the best news of all, we could afford to do this. After crunching all the numbers, we realized what God had been doing all along. Because we spent our last seven years in South Carolina working and saving, we would now be able to move back home to take care of our folks and be near our families. It has often been said, it's not doing the wrong thing, it's just not doing the right thing long enough! Well, our "long enough" had come to an end, and the riddle that God spoke to me several years ago came true! "Would you be willing to stay a little longer if you could stay forever where you want." That little longer lasted over three years, and that forever where I want is back home in Traverse City, Michigan. Final destination!

Our home in South Carolina sold in good order, and I knew that as soon as it did, we would be gone from the Carolinas very quickly. Sadly, I turned in my notice at church and began the process of sorting and packing for home. I was certainly overjoyed at moving back home, but we had become extremely attached to our friends down South. It was truly bittersweet. But God was on the move, and we were walking in tandem step with him now. I believed our house would sell by the end of July and we would be back in Michigan by the end of summer. I just knew it in my heart. And that's exactly how it happened. Just the right folks bought our place July 29 and set the closing date for the August 27. Yikes! Fortunately, I already had done a lot of the legwork regarding movers, so as soon as the house sold, everything just fell into place. Jim turned in his notice and worked right up until the end. I gave him a choice: "Do you want to pack, or do you want to work and pay for the packers." He chose the latter, and it really worked out best for us both. He could focus on training others at work to take over his responsibilities, and I could focus on the move. We had marvelous packers, and they loaded that big orange truck with our worldly possessions, which would once again go up and over the mountains to our precious Mitten State. I saved the relocation money from the move down and the cost came almost to the penny! This timing was not in my hand, it was determined by the mortgage company, the movers, and most importantly God. The day the movers put the last item in the truck was Jim's last day at work. We spent the last night in our favorite home of all homes on air mattresses, packed our cars early the next morning, and left South Carolina on August 28, our forty-second anniversary. We drove our two cars the sixteen hours back up the mountains and arrived back home in Traverse City, Michigan, on August 29, exactly forty-two years to the day we left in 1971. We could not have planned that if we tried. And the best part…the biblical numerical definition of the number 42 is "rest after many trials."

Now there was one last riddle to solve. Remember the noise in my head? Well, the noise is gone now, and all I hear is the chirping of the birds, the waves crashing on the sand, the giggles of our grandchildren, and the laughter of our parents. I asked the Lord what was that noise in my head all of those years?

I heard my Heavenly Father say, "That was your homing beacon."

Hindsight Diary 23

Epilogue

We all have an epilogue or another story. In my case, I felt I learned so much between the last chapter and the epilogue that it was worth including in this book. My biggest lesson learned was that God isn't done with any of us yet. I cut my Christian teeth in the faith movement, and my faith in Christ really helped me while living in the trenches. But if I had not learned about grace while living through my last chapter down south, I really don't think I would have been able to write the epilogue. God's grace gave me the ability to believe and relax in Christ and his love for me. It also gave me the ability to give others the grace I so badly needed myself. In this last writing of the hindsight diary, write about your story and how the grace of God has not only affected you but those whom your love.

I hope this book has helped you to distinguish between the voice of God and the lies of the enemy. If you will filter all you hear through God's word, I believe you will discern the Lord's voice clearer than the loudest roar of any lion.

Jim and I look forward to meeting you in heaven or this side of eternity.

The Invitation

Eternity waits for us all. When this earthly body passes away, our spirit will continue on forever. If you laid your head on your pillow tonight and slipped off into eternity, do you know where you will be when you wake up? If you have any doubts at all, please say this prayer with me.

Heavenly Father, I come to you in the name of Jesus. I believe that Jesus is your Son, and he died on the cross for me. Please forgive me for every sin I've ever committed. Thank you for making me new inside and out. Thank you for loving and forgiving me. In Jesus's name. Amen.

Welcome to the Kingdom of God.